Little Chef

THE

heart

OF THE

DEAL

Little Chef
THE
heart
OF THE
DEAL

LAWRENCE WOSSKOW

Library of Congress Control Number: 2017954450

ISBN Paperback: 978-1-947368-26-2
ISBN eBook: 978-1-947368-27-9

Cover Design: Chris Treccani

One-third of the author's proceeds from the sales of this book will go to Dreamflight, www.dreamflight.org, and one-third will go to the Elton John AIDS Foundation, www.ejaf.org.

CONTENTS

HEART ATTACK

"There's a good chance you're not going to make it through the night, Mr. Wosskow," the tired doctor informed me. I wanted to push her words away. Surely she was exaggerating to communicate that the situation was serious? Then she really hit home.

"I think you should contact your next of kin."

Judging from her ashen face, she was very sorry. Not nearly as sorry as I was! Nobody likes to be confronted with their mortality, least of all at short notice in an over-lit hospital emergency room, far from loved ones. Shock, panic and self-pity threatened to paralyze me. In the back of my mind, however, I had to admit that this scenario had been waiting to play itself out for a long time. I couldn't deny this; I'd brought it on myself.

Only hours before, I'd even joked about it, in a football stadium in Germany, watching the quarter-finals of the 2006 World Cup. After thirty minutes of knuckle-biting extra time, Portugal knocked my beloved England out 3-1 on penalties. At the time, I declared, "Watching that was enough to give any fan a heart attack." Well, here was the heart attack.

But the real reason wasn't watching in disbelief as we lost David Beckham to injury just after half-time, or brilliant young striker Wayne Rooney's chances of saving the match disappear after he was sent off for an irascible stomp at the nether regions of Ricardo Carvalho with a full 28 minutes to go. No. The real culprit was my lifelong search for seemingly impossible challenges and the adrenaline rush that came with them. Since I was a lad, I'd pursued one full-on adventure after another, always moving quickly to the next. Because many of these were business ventures – and highly successful ones, at that – it was easy to tell myself I was living life within the bounds of good sense. But, looking back, I know that I often chose professional challenges precisely because they came with the buzz of achieving the improbable.

The particular challenge that brought on a heart attack at the tender age of 42 was the noble quest to save the much-loved but troubled chain of British motorway service-station restaurants: Little Chef. It was such an honor to be put in charge of this iconic institution. Like millions of Brits who had grown up going on holiday in the United Kingdom, I had greeted the friendly red-and-white roadside signs for Little Chef with relief and something close to love. You knew you were going to get a rest from the road, and you knew you'd be welcomed with a cheery interior and the kind of food kids love, including chips with everything. Now, it was in financial difficulties and threatened with extinction, and I was the man who was going to save it.

I took the task very seriously. Not only had I invested a significant portion of my wealth in buying Little Chef; I'd poured my heart and soul into it, too. For months, I had worked fifteen-hour days, clocking up more than 7,000 road-miles as I personally visited 220 out of the chain's 233 restaurants, all the while with a cellphone clamped to my ear as I figured out finances, menu changes, real estate deals… a dizzying whirl of moving parts I needed to get working together like a well-conducted orchestra. Stressful as it had been, I genuinely felt I was in the home stretch – weeks away from implementing plans that would restore to glory what I considered to be a national treasure.

My heart, however, was fed up. My heart had other plans.

People ask me what it's like to have a heart attack and I tell them: the truly horrible thing about it is the symptoms can be mild at first. They're very distinctive, however, and it's crucial to be aware of them. We're all prone to dismiss health problems until they become severe, and that's certainly what I did. I'd been having mild symptoms for days, on and off, including severe indigestion in my stomach and pains in my chest. I had pushed on regardless.

I flew out from London to Germany with my friend Mark Hurley that fateful Saturday morning for the football match that was very nearly my last. I'd only known Mark for 11 years then, but he'd become as close a friend to me as the lads I grew up with. We share many traits, including an enduring love of football, which made him the perfect companion for this trip to cheer on England in the quarter-finals. As it turned out, having him on the trip was a great idea for other, grimmer reasons.

We met up with friends from all over the country in downtown Gelsenkirchen, all drinking and having a laugh before the game. When I got on the train from the city centre to the stadium, I began to feel the return of my symptoms, but blamed my discomfort on the fact that the train was unbearably hot and crowded. There was no relief, however.

Inside the stadium, the organizers had decided to leave the roof closed, and I felt strangled by the humidity. The "indigestion" was back, too. During second half and extra time, I drank ten pints of water, but I couldn't get it to subside. As the nil-nil game dragged on, I felt more and more nauseated. When it finally finished after 30 minutes of extra time and penalties, the queues to get out were horrifically long, and everyone was pushing and shoving to get out in the stifling heat. I felt panicked. Mark and I decided to jump over a fence to get out. As I landed, I noticed with alarm a new level of pain in my chest. By the time we were on the bus to the airport, I realized that something was terribly wrong. And then I did the worst thing that I could have possibly done in my situation. I got on a flight to Heathrow.

Flying while having a heart attack can make it much, much worse, because the air pressure in the cabin drops to the equivalent of 5,000–8,000 ft. above sea level, where your heart has to work harder to deliver oxygen to your blood. This is very dangerous if you already have a blockage. And I had a blockage. By the time I arrived in London, I was sweating, nauseated and suffering severe pain in my chest and left arm. The symptoms of a heart attack were finally undeniable.

It was 2 o'clock in the morning. Mark rushed me to Hillingdon Hospital, the closest healthcare facility to the airport. While the British system of free healthcare for all sounds fantastic, it can lack the infrastructure and adequate personnel to cope in a true emergency. I was unlucky enough to be admitted while the thinly spread hospital staff was frantically dealing with the aftermath of a car crash. It was therefore 5:00 a.m. before a doctor could turn her attention to me – an estimated eleven hours since the heart attack began. The delay was mostly my fault; true. But I lost a crucial three hours in that emergency ward. My ECG was abnormal, the blood tests showed a massive amount of heart damage. My chances, therefore, of surviving the night were... at best, uncertain. It was time to call my next of kin.

With a roiling mix of emotions that included a large dose of fear, I pulled out my cellphone and bolstered myself to make the hardest call I would ever have to make. Then, things took a lunatic turn.

"I'm sorry, but you can't use your cellphone in the hospital," the doctor said. "You'll have to go outside."

I was too exhausted, scared and stunned to argue. Stumbling in pain, I made my way outside to call Julie, the beautiful woman who has been my wife since I was seventeen. We had been so close for so long. She was my left arm. The thoughts that ran through my head were mostly about how she would cope without me, even though I knew she was incredibly strong and would survive somehow for my son, Toby, 14, and daughter, Hannah, 15. I also agonized about how my kids would manage. Like any young man, Toby needed a father. Hannah believed in me so much and turned to me often for advice. What would she do now?

I don't know how much of all of that actually came out during the call. What I do know is that, towards the end of our tearful exchange, a police officer who had noticed my shocking state approached.

"End the call now," he demanded, and I obeyed. Much to my shock, he lifted me up and carried me into the emergency room. "Get this man a stretcher now!" he shouted, sending staff scattering for a gurney. He probably saved my life.

At the very least, I was still alive when Julie arrived after driving like a demon for four hours from our home in Sheffield. Simply laying eyes on my love, and feeling the warmth of her hand on my brow gave me a real boost. I was grateful to be alive. I was more than grateful; I was changed.

When I talk to other people who have gone through a near-death encounter, they often say that they regretted not living life to its fullest. That's not my story. I'm lucky enough to be able to say that my life up until that ghastly night was already crammed with a multitude of amazing experiences. But the majority of my conquests and mad escapades had really been about seeking the next, crucial buzz of adrenaline. And that adrenaline had masked a lifelong, growing anxiety I almost certainly inherited. Adrenaline had kept me going all these years, distracting me from my underlying mental strain. But now it had nearly killed me. I had persistently chosen activities that would give me spectacular "wins", like turning a company around, or coming up with a brilliant new retail idea, or jumping out of airplanes, or partying with Elton John, or getting to play tennis with Andre Agassi. These were all enormously gratifying and not, in themselves, reprehensible. But my self-medicating coping mechanism had come very close to depriving me of the things that mattered to me most – my family, my friends, the glory of human connection and the beauty of the world. All of a sudden, my priorities were very, very different.

It was time to pull the plug on all this crazy work-stress and adventuring. It was time to stop. Just stop!

I finally had the time to reflect on my past and imagine my future. With regret, I knew I would have to hand over the reins at Little Chef. It would represent an end-cap on my first life, the bridge too far. I needed to live a different kind of life now, at least for a while. Fate had granted me a gift it grants very few people – a chance to lead a second life. I'd always grabbed life with both hands; now it was time to savor every minute in a different way. My family, friends and business partners all agreed I would step back from my business activities and, for me, there was some guilt, but also a lot of relief, as if I had been waiting for this to happen and slow me down. The path ahead was clear. I had enough money to lead this second part of my life in comfort. My family was on board. I had business partners I thought I could trust. I'd taken breaks from business before, especially when I was younger. But the truth is that I'd reached such a breakneck speed this time around that suddenly retiring wasn't nearly as easy as it sounds.

CHAPTER 1

I HAVE A DREAM:

JULY 5, 1987

"Lawrence, please come to my office immediately," demanded a voice down the phone in my cramped office cubicle. It was 8:00 o'clock on the morning of my 24th birthday, and the voice belonged to Jim Benfield. Since I was a junior buyer in ladies knitwear and he was director in charge of clothing at Marks & Spencer's head office on Baker Street in London, he was my boss's boss. What possible reason could he have for summoning me at this hour?

Hurriedly, I made my way to his office, which was in the well-appointed Director's wing. Ushered inside, nerves twisting my stomach in knots, I noticed the walls of his office sported beautiful photos of Mr.

1

Benfield scuba-diving in the Maldives, relishing the amazing underwater adventures his high-profile job afforded him.

Sitting with him that day was the main board director, Alan Smith, who had been a champion of mine for years. You could say he was my boss's boss's boss. He was smiling.

"In Marks & Spencer's 103 years of service, do you know how old the youngest buyer was?" Mr. Benfield asked me.

"Twenty-five," I replied.

"You know your history. I heard you were turning 24 today. How would you like to break the record and become our youngest ever buyer?" he asked. The offer was a genuine surprise; it came two years earlier than I could possibly have hoped for such a promotion. Even more impressive, it was to head up Marks & Spencer's biggest department – ladies' dresses, sets, and maternity.

This was my first taste of real success, and it only made me hungry for more. I'd been dreaming of this moment since I was a 16-year-old boy in Sheffield. The hours, days, months, and years when all my best friends were at university or working easy nine-to-five jobs while I endured a grueling, self-imposed schedule that was sometimes more like five-to-nine, never seeing daylight, had proven worthwhile. Enthusiastically, I said yes. I was elated to have reached such a significant benchmark so early in life.

And yet, within a week, I decided to leave.

That may sound crazy, but I realized that I had achieved my first real life goal and it was time to move on. No-one was more keenly aware of how hard I had been working. I also knew how well I was doing at M&S, and that the management there saw me as someone with real potential. But for me, success has always meant doing my own thing rather than thriving inside someone else's hierarchy. I wanted to succeed on my own. The weekend after this spectacular promotion, I found myself obsessively listening to a track by my favorite band, Queen – "I

Want to Break Free." With a full heart, I sang along. Then I went to a bookshop in Covent Garden and bought a map of the world. Across the top, I wrote, in big letters: "I want to break free!" I put it on my bedroom wall. I marked out everywhere I wanted to go in the world, spanning the globe with my marker pen. I had a dream. I longed to see the world. For me, it was time to break free.

Thankfully, I had a wonderful girlfriend who shared my dream.

Julie, the love of my life, came across my path one night when I was seventeen. I was sitting at home in Sheffield when a friend called me from a phone box in The Hare and Hounds pub in a local village. Over the din, I heard his cheeky enthusiasm.

"You've got to get over here and check out this girl's arse!" he said.

As my friend knew only too well, I'd always loved girls' behinds. I still do. I jumped on the bus straight away. Pushing my way into the pulsing rabble of The Hare and Hounds on a Friday night, I found the target – the most perfect bottom I'd ever seen.

It belonged to Julie. I was smitten.

She had a boyfriend. He didn't last long. Julie would be among the first to tell you that my ability to form quick and enduring personal connections, along with a healthy dose of native charm, is one of my most powerful personal traits.

I was delighted to find that a perfect bum was only one of Julie's many wonderful attributes. She was drop-dead gorgeous, but wasn't exploiting it in a calculating way like so many other pretty girls. I quickly got to know that she was kind and caring. She was not perfect, and could be shy to the point of naiveté. Mostly, I think, she was seeking stability, and offered in return a sharing, loving heart. It was a great match. After an emotionally rocky childhood during which I bore witness to my parents' tumultuous marriage and subsequent divorce, I was relieved and grateful to find a person to love, trust, do everything with, and whom I could talk to about anything. I've never looked anywhere else. She's been the one rock of stability in my life. I can safely say, 35 years later, that it was the luckiest break I ever had. Her love settled me down and allowed me to achieve so many accomplishments in life.

I must say, though, life has worked out very nicely for Julie as well. What a life she has led! People ask me if I believe in reincarnation. I always respond, "I'm not sure, but if there is such a thing, there's only one person I would choose to come back as: Julie!"

Julie and me, in the early days before the grey hairs set in!

Marks & Spencer didn't want me to leave, and I got my first real taste of how a negotiation can go if one side is genuinely prepared to walk away. It was to prove a very valuable lesson in my coming years as a business entrepreneur. I wasn't trying to leverage M&S; I honestly wanted to leave as respectfully as I could. But they offered me the moon. First, they wanted to send me to New York to help with the Brooks Brothers acquisition. When I declined that offer, they told me I could work at the office of the chairman, Lord Rayner – a unique offer that had never been made before. Lord Rayner and I had met back in Leeds; he spent an hour and 15 minutes out of his 2-hour visit talking to me. We really hit it off. But, much as I respected him, I didn't want to work for him. Or anyone else, for that matter. My mind was set. I left my job.

My mum couldn't believe it. She had a whole room full of Marks & Spencer memorabilia; she was so proud of her son. My dad couldn't get his head around it either. But none of that mattered to Julie and me.

Julie and I spent the summer selling handbags at the local London markets and making more money than I was getting paid at Marks & Spencer. We quickly saved enough to buy backpacks and go and see the world.

Many people talk about it, but few actually leave an amazing job, fill a backpack, and travel to far-flung parts of the world for two years. Working at Marks & Spencer had awoken my dormant wanderlust. A huge portion of the buying business was moving to the Far East; China was opening up for trade, and there were all these Asian countries making fabric. I wanted to see them for myself.

But not before getting in one last bit of trouble. In September, the month before we set off, I bought an old car that might as well have been a flying machine. One weekend, I was driving down the motorway from Sheffield to London with the car full of handbags I was selling. And of course I didn't have insurance for transporting them.

A police car pulled me up and asked, "Why do you think I pulled you up?"

"Well, I think I was going a bit fast," I said.

"Fast?" he exclaimed. "That was the fastest thing I've seen all year!"

When I went to court, the policeman said I was driving in excess of 125 miles per hour. He claimed he'd been chasing me for 15 miles. I had no idea whether it really happened, but the court banned me from driving for a month. But it didn't matter because, by the time the ban was enacted, we were leaving on a jet plane.

We went all around the world, starting with China. That nation had been completely closed to tourists until 1974, when Deng Xiaoping decided to promote tourism as a means of earning foreign exchange. At the time we went, only 100 locations were accessible with a visa alone; the remaining locales required travel permits from public security departments – not exactly a warm welcome. But we explored widely all the same, taking our chances and dodging the government agents who were no doubt trying to follow our every move. In one village, we were the first white people they had ever seen. We had hundreds of villagers coming up to us, feeling our faces, our clothing, and our shoes. It was truly weird to be so foreign, to know that the people all around us had never even imagined something as exotic as Julie's cagoule!

China made a big impression on my growing business entrepreneur's mind. Even then, it was clear to me that, one day, China would be a superpower on a par with the USA. Although it was a Communist country, everyone – from the man in the field who had to pick his carrots in the morning and sat on the street selling them in the afternoon, to the guy who illegally changed money on the foreign exchange markets for us – was a hardworking capitalist. India, on the other hand, obviously had the potential to be a global superpower along with America and China, but I predicted it would never reach its full potential because there were so many different religions, castes, and conflicting dogmas to contend with. Unlike China, which had a disciplined government, there was too much disorder in India's system of governing.

We arrived in Hong Kong on the day of the 1987 stock market crash and witnessed the chaotic exodus that followed. We lounged on now-destroyed pieces of paradise in Thailand. We dodged bullets on the Burmese/Vietnamese border. We hitchhiked to Ayres Rock. We rode the bullet train to Hiroshima. In many of the more remote places, we were the first Westerners to visit. It was exhilarating and wonderful.

One of many adventures

Eventually, we headed for Los Angeles, which I immediately loved for its spirit of business innovation. Julie adored it too. It seemed to me that the West Coast was where ideas and businesses started, before migrating to the East Coast and eventually crossing the ocean to the UK. So it was a feeding ground for great ideas for me, an English entrepreneur looking towards my future. After tasting the American dream, we knew that California would be part of our future.

By the end of our two-year jaunt, I was completely ready for my next phase in life. I'd had the most incredible professional training at Marks & Spencer that one could ask for. I'd been fortunate enough to see some of the great wonders of the world. I had learnt a great deal about life while travelling. And I knew what happens during a negotiation when one of the parties is willing to walk away. I was in a perfect position to begin my life as a hard-driving entrepreneur.

CHAPTER 2

THE ENTREPRENEUR UNLEASHED

I f you had to pick a location in which to begin a trailblazing career as a business innovator, I doubt Belize would spring to mind. Most people have a hard time even placing it on a map, and there is an enduringly popular tee-shirt that says, "Where the hell is Belize?" on the front, and, "Who cares?" on the back.

However, Julie and I had received a glowing recommendation from someone we met while camping in New Orleans, right at the end of our two-year journey around the world. We were both excited by the prospect of this exotic locale that neither of us had even heard of, so we went there.

The piece of land that started it all, our first deal

Belize is full of natural beauty, from its jaguars and underground rivers to its coral reefs and rich rain forests. It's a former British colony, so English is the official language, and those tangled jungles had been used as training grounds for the British military.

We found ourselves drawn to Placencia, a peninsula in the south, rimmed by emerald seas and sixteen miles of white, fine, sandy beaches. It turned out we had an opportunity to buy some of that gorgeous beachfront; a parcel of land was up for sale for £16,000. We'd never bought property before, so we were both very excited. We didn't have £16,000, but were able to borrow £15,000 from Barclay's Bank in Belize City as long as we put in £1,000 of our own money. The deal was done. Our first!

We immediately put the land up for sale with an estate agent in Belize and flew to Miami to enjoy some time on the beach there before returning to the UK. A few weeks later, out of the blue, we got a call from a guy with a northern English accent you could have grated cheese with. He had recently been on holiday in Belize, the agent had shown him our land, and he thought it would be perfect for building a beachfront hotel where he could eventually retire.

"I want that piece of land you bought in Belize. I'm not prepared to give you any more than £70,000 for it," he said.

"I don't think we can do that. I'll check with my wife," I said. Like I said, I'd learned more than interpreting sales forecasts at Marks & Spencer. A few hours later, after we'd quaffed a good few glasses of celebratory champagne, I rang him back and told him we would do the deal. Just like that, our first purchase had paid off – and then some!

Around that time, I decided to revisit an old love, and reacquainted myself with the football scene. I didn't know then that football was about to deliver one of its many messages about life and how serious things can get.

It was April 1989, and my sister Karen's boyfriend, Gaetano, and I had tickets to the semi-finals between Nottingham Forest and Liverpool at Hillsborough.

When we walked past the Leppings Lane end at 2:10 p.m., there was already chaos outside. Because that entrance was blocked, we had to walk past the Kop and Nottingham Forest end to the South Stand. At that point, the queues for the Kop entrance were very orderly. It seemed weird. Upon entering the stadium at the South Stand at 2:45 p.m., I remarked to Gaetano that the Leppings Lane central section looked dangerously full.

By the time the game kicked off at 3:00 p.m., that central section at the Leppings Lane end was more packed than I'd ever seen in all my years of attending football matches, including traveling to 90 league grounds. That's why it was clear madness to open a gate into the central section to allow even more fans in from the crush outside, and yet that's exactly what the police did that day. They made a terrible decision, and ninety-six Liverpool supporters died, crushed and suffocated against each other and the barriers that separated the spectators from the pitch. It took 27 years for an inquest to finally return a verdict of unlawful killings. It's not my role to examine the horrors of that day or the cover-up that followed. But I will tell you that what I saw that day will live with me forever. I was on the pitch for 90 minutes helping to get people clear and carry the injured out on makeshift stretchers made from torn-down advert hoardings – grim work.

In later years, I became close friends with King Kenny – Kenny Dalglish, the Liverpool manager who became the shining light of Hillsborough. He helped the 96 families who lost loved ones, and the 766 who were injured in what is still the worst disaster in British sporting history. King Kenny attended all the funerals, and lived through every single last second of the ordeal, which will stay with him and his lovely wife Marina for the remainder of their lives.

What I learned that day, through the trauma of witnessing so many losing their lives up close, was how important it is to help people. It must be done without calculating what reward you'll get, too. That's crucial. I think many people believe successful entrepreneurs get to be that way by taking advantage of those around them and looking to get ahead at the expense of others. But I feel it's important to honor the humanity of those around you and to recognize the times when you simply must offer whatever you can to help those in need.

Nevertheless, this attitude has brought me some incredible benefits over time and has become one of my core principles, not only in my personal life, but also in business. I'm ambitious and I play hardball, but I'm not in the least bit interested in crushing my business rivals, or taking anyone to the cleaners, or any such Gordon Gekko-like nonsense. Good business is when all the parties involved make money. It's really that simple. It can't always work out that way, especially over the long term, but that's the goal. If I can, I like to help people.

One early lesson in the benefits of being helpful in business came in London, shortly after I settled there. I was asked to help a guy who had started a business displaying ties in dry cleaner's shops, selling them on concession. After two days, I told him I couldn't help anymore; I didn't think it was a very good business venture.

He liked me all the same, and wanted to return the favour, so he offered to introduce me to his friend, Roger Myers, who had recently set up a restaurant chain called Pelican Group with three outlets: one Cafe Pelican and two Café Rouges.

Roger and I hit it off immediately, and he had a business proposition for me. "If you're prepared to put £50,000 in and buy some shares in the company," he said, "you can be part of the future of my business."

The timing could not have been more fortuitous. With £70,000 coming in from the Belize deal, I could pay the bank back the £15,000 I owed on the original purchase, and still have £55,000 left over to invest. I had nothing else in the world, but the numbers looked good and, as a great believer in fate, I decided this was the deal to go for. Roger's small public limited company was about to acquire a fourth restaurant in Highgate, London. For this, he was paying with shares in the Pelican Group. In line with the deal, I agreed to buy shares at 25p each – £50,000 worth, which was pretty much all the profit from Belize.

Within a week the Highgate deal was done, but Roger made a critical error by forgetting to put in a "no-sell" clause that forbade the buyers from selling the shares for a year. Many of the investors immediately dumped their shares in Café Rouge and their value dropped from 25p to 11p that week. My £50,000 went down to £20,000 overnight. Not a good start!

But Julie and I were enjoying living in London. I was getting paid a good salary at the Pelican Group, and it was expanding like mad. I began to learn the restaurant business and put my own training scheme in place, copying what I had learned at Marks & Spencer from the bottom up. A few weeks later, I took over site selection and buying. Café Rouge was trading really well and we were opening a new restaurant every week. The shares went from 25p to 35p to 50p to 70p. It turned out to be a very good start, after all.

I was settling into my new role at Café Rouge, enjoying being involved in the hottest restaurant chain in London, when Julie woke me one morning with some major news.

"I'm pregnant," she announced. "I want to move back to Sheffield to have the baby."

"That's kind of tough right now. We're involved in Café Rouge and everything we have is tied up in it."

"I don't care. I want to move back," she said.

We had always agreed that she would choose where we lived, which proved to be the right decision for all our lives. Regretfully, I resigned from my position at Café Rouge but kept my shares, which had hit 75p at this point.

We moved back to Sheffield, rented a house, and started selling handbags at the markets again. As we earned money, we reinvested in

Café Rouge shares each time there was a rights issue. Under that deal, they'd value our shares at a pound and split them into 50p shares.

When Café Rouge shares grew north of 120p, I had the feeling an offer would not be far away. I was right. Whitbread came in and paid £140 million for what was then the fastest-growing restaurant business the UK had ever seen.

It was great, because when Hannah, our first child, was born, I had the chance to spend loads of time with her; it's probably the reason we're so close. I'll never forget the night she was born. My mates and I wet the baby's head big time. We went out and painted the town red. Knowing that Julie would be in the hospital for a while after her Caesarian, we wrecked the house. It was rented, we were drunk, and we didn't care. We smashed windows. My friend Shirty stole the kettle, and worst of all I ran out of money playing cards and gambled away the dining room table and chairs, losing them to another vagabond, Moycee! The place was a mess.

The following morning, Julie called with good news: "I'm coming home with Hannah tonight."

Of course, Julie *would* have a speedier recovery than expected; she's such a strong woman. She'll undoubtedly get a letter from the Queen when she turns one hundred. So we had one day to get the place together before she arrived. Both my mum and Julie's knew I was in trouble and they helped us clean up the house just in time.

Months later, Julie called me crying. She had arrived home to find a "sold" sign on the house we were renting. The landlord gave us 28 days to get out. Luckily, my accountant, Paul Dawson, and I had seen a wrecked house for sale. He introduced me to the manager at HSBC Bank, whose regional office was in Sheffield. He lent us some money and we used part of the money from the Café Rouge sale to purchase our first house in Sheffield.

A year later, Toby was born. I had said all the way through Julie's pregnancy that I was not bothered if we had a girl or a boy, as long as the baby was healthy. Deep inside, I admit, I wanted a boy, and that dream came true. However, after bringing Hannah home from visiting her brother in the hospital for the first time, I noticed she had chicken pox. Sadly, baby Toby caught it too, so Julie and Toby had to stay in the hospital for a week longer than we expected. This time, we did not wet the baby's head!! We were just full of joy when he made a full recovery and we were all at home together.

So now we had a house and two kids, but I didn't know what my next professional move would be. I wanted to use the remaining money from selling my Café Rouge shares to buy a business. I attempted to buy several, getting to final bids on two or three that fell through at the last minute. Those were deals, I concluded, that weren't meant to be, but I learned a lot from pursuing them.

Finally, the deal that took me to the next level emerged, but it wasn't an easy win, and required all the skills of charm and persuasion I could muster. Funnily enough, the idea came from my beloved mum; she suggested I approach the owner of Bradwell's Ice Cream and offer to buy the business.

I knew and loved Bradwell's Ice Cream. My mum used to take me to the shop in Derbyshire, near Sheffield, to eat their delicious wares when I was a kid. It turned out the owner, moreover, lived next door, and he became a family friend. Now, he was retiring. "It'd be perfect for you," Mum said. Since it was a brand name with a ton of local recognition and admiration, I agreed with her. Bradwell's had a long history, dating back to before refrigeration when Hannah Bradwell brought the ice in from Sheffield by train and made the ice cream just for the local people of Bradwell. I believed it had enormous growth potential under the right hands. It really did sound perfect.

But, as it turned out, it wasn't that simple. Noel Bradwell, the grandson of the founder, Hannah Bradwell, was retiring all right. But he had absolutely no intention of selling the business to anyone.

"The village is called Bradwell. My family's called Bradwell. The ice cream is called Bradwell's. It's dying with me," he declared when I went to see him. "I'm going to close it down now. That'll be the end of it."

In all the business negotiations I've ever conducted, I've applied the same principle – look to find what it is the seller really wants. Because he was a family friend and we had spent time together, I knew that he knew me to be a sincere and trustworthy person. By the same token, I knew that what really concerned him was the danger of the family name being sullied in some way. His fear was that he'd be walking down the street in a few years' time and see low-quality ice cream full of vegetable fat and artificial flavours for sale under the Bradwell's name. He would have shamed three generations of Bradwells. So I did something you're not supposed to do in business; I offered the seller the option to take back control of the business in one year if he didn't like what I was doing with it. He would retain the brand name and I'd just sell the buildings and equipment for whatever I could get. He would lose nothing. It was a deal he couldn't turn down, because it gave him the chance to see the Bradwell's name carry on in a way he approved of. It turned out to be a marriage made in heaven. Noel and I became best friends. He referred to me as the son he never had. He even came out of retirement to help in the factory. At the time, the business had a turnover of £90,000. I relished the opportunity to go out and turn this tiny business into a well-known brand.

The press had a field day with my takeover. To some, I was this audacious whippersnapper who had been Marks & Spencer's youngest-ever buyer and a director at Pelican Group and the Café Rouge chain, who had now moved back up north to shake up an ice cream business that had been sleepy since 1899. To others, I was a home-grown, local entrepreneur swooping in to rescue a much-cherished local business about to be shuttered.

At the time, Häagen-Dazs was entering the market with sexy advertising that depicted beautiful women rubbing ice cream all over their bodies. I thought to myself, "What could we do as a small, northern ice cream maker?" In those days, there was a very popular TV sitcom set not far away in West Yorkshire, called "Last of the Summer Wine". One of the most famous characters was Nora Batty, a stern northern battle-axe, permanently dressed in a pinny, a scraggy cardigan and hair curlers – no beauty! I jokingly told the press that I planned to approach Nora Batty with the proposition that she be our model and smear Bradwell's ice cream all over herself. They ate it up like a tub of Raspberry Ripple! Of course, I was only joking, but the publicity was fantastic.

To make ends meet while I figured out how to make the ice cream business hum, Julie continued to sell handbags at markets in Sheffield. It was hard work, making, selling and delivering ice cream while running this other business. The days were long. One afternoon, I got to the market with the van, opened up the back door to put all the handbags in and realized I had forgotten to put the ice cream back in the freezer at the factory. The van was just about to run out of chill. I was in a bind.

Luckily, there was a big Somerfield food store nearby. I knew they'd have huge freezers with plenty of space, if only I could convince them to help me. I went in, explained my situation to the manager and pleaded with him to store all the ice cream overnight. Somehow, my pleading worked. The next day, when I went to collect all that mercifully still-frozen ice cream, I told him that, one day, his food store chain of hundreds of outlets would being stacking up Bradwell's at the front of the store, not the back. He was doubtful. It gave me great pleasure when, a mere 12 months later, this actually came true.

The newspaper stories began to lead to bigger sales, and the business expanded rapidly. It was a nice problem to have, but I knew that, even if the factory was able to keep up with demand, the area around the factory wouldn't be big enough to store all the ice cream we'd be making. About five miles up the road was the biggest frozen food distributor in the area – Holdsworth Foods. They had gone from selling frozen chickens in 1969 to becoming one of the major suppliers of chilled and frozen food to the catering industry in the UK now. I reckoned they might have some freezer space to rent, and when I met up with the founder and chairman, Michael Holdsworth, I quickly found I was right. He readily agreed to let us store our Bradwell's ice cream in his freezers for a reasonable fee. But, of course, I wanted to push for more. I wanted the thrill of a really big win.

I asked him to take on Bradwell's as one of the brands he supplied. You have to understand; this represented a huge – almost unimaginable – increase in volume. Plus, of course, we'd already approached him through normal sales channels. Here I was, trying to switch one kind of very minor business arrangement as a customer into a much more lucrative one as a supplier. Luckily, my cheekiness didn't put him off. He knew what it was to build a business from scratch. Firmly, however, he declined the offer.

"I didn't want your ice cream before; why would I want it now?" he replied.

"Who's your current supplier?" I asked.

"Lyons Maid," he said. That was the second biggest ice cream business in Britain at the time, maker of the famous Zoom ice lolly.

I grinned because I knew something he didn't.

"Lyons Maid is going out of business," I said.

"That's impossible!" he argued.

It wasn't just possible; it was a certainty. The thing I knew that Michael Holdsworth didn't was that Lyons Maid was having trouble paying its suppliers. I knew this because I happened to buy packaging for Bradwell's ice cream from the same company that supplied Lyons

Maid. The owner of the packaging company, Tim Parker, was a really nice guy, and we became good friends. One day, he took me into his confidence – Lyons Maid had stopped paying on time. It was clear they were in trouble.

"Okay," said Mr. Holdsworth. "If Lyons Maid goes out of business, you can have all their orders the next day." He actually laughed dismissively at the absurdity of the idea of such a huge company going out of business.

But, sure as ice cream melts, the front page of the following Monday's *Financial Times* was dominated by a story about how Lyons Maid was going out of business.

Clutching the paper, I waited three hours outside Michael Holdsworth's office while he was in meetings. When I finally gained entrance, I silently put the *Financial Times* down in front of him. He gave a different laugh now, a friendly one. He'd seen the paper earlier and knew a visit from me wouldn't be far behind. He was true to his word. He gave me the business. "This is your break," he said. "Make the most of it."

It was a break, all right. Suddenly, Bradwell's turnover needed to jump 400 percent! We weren't ready, but we coped. We desperately needed reliable managers. I was lucky enough to recruit Mark Bownes and Simon Allot to work alongside Jane Fox. Jane and Mark got married years later, and those three loyal people still run the business today.

The first season was absolute chaos. We built extra freezers quickly. We couldn't get boxes with our label made in time, so we bought the only boxes available, which turned out to be pizza boxes. Obviously, we hadn't quite thought that one through – try fitting ice cream into flat, square pizza boxes! But somehow, we figured it out. We worked very hard in challenging circumstances.

When I was brainstorming with Jane about how to make Bradwell's more popular, she had the idea that it would be fun and lucrative to have an ice cream van. So I bought one cheap. It was so old, it was covered in Smurfs, but we painted over those. We managed to secure a great site at a famous local beauty spot – the stepping stones at Dovedale, which is a spectacular limestone ravine filled with wild flowers and lush woodlands, complete with huge stepping stones that allow you to cross the sparkling river. It's near Ashbourne in the Peak District National Park and attracts huge numbers of visitors, many of whom, of course, would just love an ice cream to complete their visit. Because it was a National Park, we had to be very respectful. Part of the contract contained a clause that limited sales to ice cream and cones only, so that there would be no litter.

One hot Sunday, Julie, Hannah, Toby, and I drove to the stepping stones to check out our latest venture. I was delighted to find, upon arrival, a queue of thirty customers for our van. But when I got closer, my heart sank. The staff had no intention of honoring the contract. They were selling sandwiches, cans of drinks and sweets – all with wrappers that were ending up all over the place. Worse, one of the two guys working behind the counter was stuffing his face with the biggest ice cream I had ever seen. Part of me admired their entrepreneurship, but I knew they could get me in trouble with the Peak District National Park authorities. They were also stealing, of course. So I fired them both on the spot and Julie, the kids, and I took over. I drove the ice cream van back to Bradwell's factory later while Julie followed me in the car, reflecting that the thing about running your own business is that, truly, you never quite know what you're going to find yourself doing next. A day in the countryside can turn into an afternoon frantically selling ice creams from a van.

I have no idea how those two rascals got home. What I do know is that a call from Jane to both their parents landed them in very hot water indeed.

When the euphoria of my dazzling expansion had receded a bit, I realized the obvious issue with UK ice cream distribution – it was, to say the least, seasonal. We had huge sales in the summer and virtually no sales in the winter. But I noticed that the retail environment in the UK was shifting. Up until then, everything had been sold in in the city centre. Britain was a solidly High Street retail environment. But a forward-looking Yorkshire property entrepreneur called Eddie Healey had recently taken over a piece of land near the motorway that used to be a steelworks, and on that land, he had built the biggest shopping centre in Europe, called – somewhat ironically, given its industrial origins – Meadowhall. It was a breath-takingly audacious move – a million and a half square feet of shopping paradise, air-conditioned in the summer, heated in the winter, packed with bars and shops aplenty. It was a sensation.

By this point, I knew retail quite well, and I had observed that most retail sales, although not ice cream, are made through October, November, December, and January, when the weather is – frankly – bloody awful. I thought that if I could put ice cream inside the shopping centres, like they did in the US, we'd get people to buy ice cream in the winter months, when everybody's out spending money. There were already 24 million people a year shopping at Meadowhall. With my ambitious plan dancing in my head, I approached the management.

"You've got all these shops paying rent on the outside, but you've got all this space in the middle with nothing there," I reasoned. "I want to put ice cream carts into your shopping centre. It won't take away from anybody else's business. Ice cream is an impulse buy, like when a child passes and begs her mum for one," I said, with all the confidence in the world.

"It's a good idea, but I don't know if we'll do it," said the man who took my meeting.

You could hardly blame him for his hesitancy. No-one else was doing this, and he wasn't the type of man who wanted to risk being first at anything. But I knew his boss, Eddie Healey, was. He was a trailblazer. He was also a real Yorkshireman who would appreciate my bravado.

I took out my cheque book, ripped out a cheque and signed it, blank. His eyes widened in surprise as I handed it to him. "Go and give this to your boss," I said, smiling reassuringly. "Tell him to fill in the amount he wants per month for four ice cream carts." I was prepared with a map of Meadowhall. I marked the places in the shopping centre where I wanted to set my carts. His whole body language changed. He obviously thought I was a big deal. Little did he know I was making a massive gamble. But it seemed to me, the down side was minimal compared to the potential reward. It's not the last time I've made that kind of calculation over an audacious proposition. In business, as in life, it's pretty much always worth asking for what you actually want, even if it seems extremely unlikely. You'd be surprised how often the answer is yes! And yet many people temper their expectations in anticipation of being turned down. That's not my style at all.

The gamble paid off. The following week, I was asked back to the centre to meet with Eddie Healey. The deal was on. It turned out to be the beginning of a very fruitful relationship. We put four carts in Meadowhall on October 1, 1994, and sales immediately went through the roof. At times, the queues were so long, we had to have four staff for each cart. All of a sudden, Bradwell's had a four-season business, with year-round cash flow. I was proud to say that Bradwell's was the third best-selling food product in the shopping centre, behind Coca-Cola and McDonald's.

When I was building the Bradwell's Ice Cream cart business, I also put a cart selling pick-n-mix sweets into Meadowhall, and that was a great success, too. Because of getting into that line of business, I met a man from Scarborough who made gumball machines. I liked the idea of seeing how far we could push those. I put a few, initially, in local theme parks and they were a huge success. On the back of that, I won a one-year contract with the supermarket chain ASDA for 150 of their stores. The man from Scarborough sold me £80,000-worth of gumball machines and dutifully delivered them to the stores.

But at the end of that year, I received my first hard lesson about business: Just because you're a straight dealer, doesn't mean everyone you do business with is too. For no apparent reason, ASDA told me they were not renewing the contract. When I dug into it, I found out why. The guy from Scarborough had gone behind my back and offered ASDA a higher rent. And if you're wondering how he could afford to do that, the phone call I received from him very shortly after will explain it quite clearly. He was going to stiff me on the machines.

He said, "Remove the 150 machines yourself, or I'll buy them from you for £10,000." Those machines cost £80,000 just a year ago – quite a bargain. For him! But he knew only too well that removing the machines would have cost me a fortune, so I opted to sell. Someone more bloody-minded than me might have gotten the machines removed and trashed them, just for spite. Truly, I was really annoyed with him, but I was also grateful for the lesson he taught me, harsh as it was. He had a lot more experience and was more cut-throat than I was. I learned from him that you must always be on the lookout for someone who can undercut you.

Despite this setback, my efforts were paying off beautifully. Bradwell's was becoming a *bona fide* business, with turnover of £2 million a year. But for me, it wasn't enough that half a million people every year were trying our ice cream while they were out and about. I wanted to get it into their homes. My experience at Marks & Spencer was useful, as were my powers of persuasion, and I managed to get Bradwell's into the major supermarket chains – Sainsbury's, Tesco and Morrisons all jumped on board. The business was flourishing, thanks in part to the diligence and imagination of Jane Bownes. I quickly promoted her to managing director.

My background in retail was really coming to the fore, and one mall wasn't enough. I wanted to get ice cream carts into the UK's other famous shopping centre – the MetroCentre near Newcastle, which had opened in 1986 with more than 2 million square feet of retail space. I succeeded at this in 1995. That year, Bradwell's won the HSBC Business of the Year Award, and I went to their head office in London to collect the award.

At that point, my inner entrepreneur had truly come of age, and was fully unleashed. I began breaking my way into malls throughout the country. It seemed there was no limit to what I could achieve, and the rush was incredible.

CHAPTER 3

THE ROAD TO LITTLE CHEF

Selling ice cream year-round from carts in shopping malls was not a new idea – they'd been doing it in America for years. But it was a huge novelty to the Brits. It's hard to picture now what a massive change it was for British people to get used to the idea of shopping malls – or shopping centres, as we know them.

Even though the first urban shopping centres had opened in the mid-60s, in London, Birmingham and Liverpool, and then out-of-town shopping centres began to emerge in the mid-70s, these early attempts at revolutionizing retail in the UK quickly developed reputations as thoroughly depressing places to shop. The Bull Ring in Birmingham, for example, chose an ill-conceived layout that attempted to reproduce the arrangement of the streets it replaced, giving shoppers a confusing sensation of being bounced around a maze of concrete. Often there were more boarded-up shop fronts than open ones, especially on the upper floors. Worse, they attracted vandalism, as the same shelter out of the wind and the rain that was supposed to appeal to shoppers also attracted young layabouts. Shoppers didn't want merely an indoor version of the High Street; they wanted something they hadn't seen before. Meadowhall was a whole different proposition. Light and airy, with a combination of High Street and designer shops, it came much closer to the brightly energetic vibe of shopping malls already commonplace in America. It had air conditioning in the summer, for the rare times it was needed and – far more critically – was heated in the winter, maintaining a balmy year-round temperature of 23°C. It was an environment, a day's holiday, an adventure.

And a great place to be licking a delicious ice cream while window-shopping.

As our Bradwell's carts really took off in Meadowhall and the MetroCentre, I realized that our logo needed a major facelift. The old-fashioned tubs had no color, making it almost impossible to distinguish the flavors. We had already designed a great look for the ice cream carts – a photo of my daughter, Hannah, eating an ice cream, taken just before her second birthday. Everybody loved it. All the kids in the shopping centre saw a little girl eating our ice cream and wanted one. We changed the packaging on the tubs to match. People recognized the branding instantly when they went into the supermarket or local shop, so they bought a tub to take home. It was a terrific choice for branding, because it was the only ice cream with a little girl on it – incredibly distinctive.

Hannah, the ice cream girl

Hannah, of course, loved it at the time. What little girl doesn't want to be a superstar? But three years later, she came home from school crying. She said the kids at school were making fun of her for the being the Bradwell's Ice Cream girl. The father in me won out over the businessman. Obviously, I couldn't bear to see one of my children suffer.

I immediately had a new logo designed and, over a short period of time, replaced Hannah on all the tubs.

When she turned 12, however, the idea of celebrity began to appeal to her again. She came to me and said, "Dad, was I once on the ice cream tubs and all the things having to do with Bradwell's Ice Cream?"

"Yes, you were," I told her.

"Why did you take me off?" she asked.

"Because you begged me to," I said, with a sinking feeling about what was coming next.

"Well, I want to be on them again!" she demanded.

There's a Hollywood adage that advises: Never work with dogs or children.

"Darling," I explained calmly. "It cost me £25,000 to take you off once. And it would cost me even more money to put you back on." I'm still not sure she's entirely let go of the idea.

Making the Bradwell's brand soar gave me a terrific high, as did my increasing interest in outdoor sports that pumped my adrenaline ever higher. That, in turn, guided my next adventure – into outdoor-themed retail. There was a shop in Meadowhall called Free Spirit that focused on hiking, climbing, and cycling. I loved the name and the concept. Free Spirit effectively introduced surfing brands before surfing became important in the UK. Most of the stores in the mall were geared towards women, but Free Spirit was a true Man Cave, where guys could go to check out athletic equipment and watch sports while their partners went shopping for a couple of hours.

The Free Spirit storefront

I thought it would be a great business to buy, so I approached the store's owner, Nick Smith, in 1996, and we cut a deal. I was thrilled. My delight lasted four weeks, until Eddie Healey called me in to a meeting. My favorite entrepreneur looked very serious indeed. He said, "You bought the wrong store. I need that space."

Eddie Healey is a tough cookie. He and his brother, Malcolm, both left school at 16 with no qualifications and started out in their father's Hull-based DIY company. Now, between them, they're estimated to be worth £1.45 billion. Over the years that I've been lucky enough to call him a friend and mentor, he's taught me to show respect to those in powerful positions that can influence your life, as well as the art of doing deals. I was about to get one of my first lessons from him.

Unbeknownst to me, Eddie had been negotiating with all the retailers in that part of Meadowhall to move them so he could put in a huge retail outlet for Next, one of the most successful fashion clothing and homeware stores in Britain at the time. Now, I presented an obstacle.

Seeing only the injustice in his demand, I pushed back hard.

"You can't have it. I've got a fifteen-year lease," I said.

Eddie wasn't going to let a little thing like a signed lease get in the way of what he wanted.

"I'll put it like this, Lawrence. If I don't get it, I'm going to put Millets on one side of you, and Blacks on the other side of you," he said. Millets and Blacks were my two biggest competitors and much larger than Free Spirit in the U.K. I would be dead in the water.

As if it needed explaining, he added, "I will destroy your business."

"Are you serious?" I asked. This was like a scene from *Goodfellas*.

"Dead serious," he said.

I'd just parted with half a million pounds to buy the Free Spirit business. Now I was going to let him simply take it off me?

"You're going to make me go bankrupt," I said.

"No I'm not," he said. "I'm going to do two things. I'll give you another shop in the shopping centre where I don't need the space, and I'll pay for the fit-out so you've got another store you can just move into."

It wasn't ideal, but at least it was something.

"The second thing is – and I'm going to write this down in my little notebook – in years to come, you'll get paid back."

I had no choice. We moved the store. Eddie Healey was as good as his word. A few years later, he did me a very large favor indeed. You'll learn about that later.

Sheffield at the time was not short of entrepreneurs, and five of us, supposedly intelligent businessmen, formed a lunch club called The 1k Investment Club. The idea was that we would each choose a business in which to invest £1,000 and see how brilliant we were. The team was allegedly great. I joined Paul Dawson, who became senior partner of Hart Shaw, one of Sheffield's leading accountants, a supposed businessman; David Grey, a great businessman who went on to become

Sheffield's Master Cutler; and George, who was salt of the earth, and a concrete specialist.

Well, we soon renamed it The 1k Plummet Club.

We all took in turns to choose the lunch venue and pick up the bill. When it was George's turn, he chose a Chinese restaurant. We had just arrived at the *piece de resistance*, the Peking duck, when George excused himself and got up to take a phone call. When he didn't come back, we assumed either the food or the bill was too rich for him!

It turned out the concrete truck had broken down and he was too late to fix the problem; the whole load had set inside the truck. It took him all night to dig it out. It seemed a perfect metaphor for exactly what had happened with my investment, and I pulled out, duck or no duck. This episode of playing the stock market taught me so much. I learned to invest in myself, not the stock market, where everyone is playing with everyone else's money but their own.

George was a rare type and always up to something. One day, around this time, he asked me for five thousand pounds. I asked him why. He said he'd been reading about wine and wanted to invest in it seriously, but needed someone to go 50/50 in it with him. I said yes, I gave him the money, and off he went.

Three months later, he approached me again and said he needed £250 now. Again, I asked why. It was for two dehumidifiers to keep the wine in optimum storage conditions. Fine, I gave him the £250. Then, a few days later, he rang me *again*. The guy who had sold him the humidifiers also had two white Rolls Royces for sale and, on impulse, George had bought them both. People were always after white Rolls Royces for brides to make elegant entrances and exits at their weddings. It seemed like a fantastic opportunity to him. He told me he wouldn't be around for the summer, as he had 30 weddings already lined up. What a character! He was no flake, either. Two years later – lo and behold! – he delivered to me £10,000 and a lot of valuable wine.

My approach to making money, aside from the odd flutter on a friend, was much more methodical, of course. It was around this time, in 1995, that I learned Loseley Ice Cream, the southern equivalent of Bradwell's, had gone into administration. It was a natural fit for my business and I wanted it!

There were, however, quite a few other people who were interested as well. So I went down to Birmingham where the administrator was based and stayed there, trying to come to terms, until two in the morning. Finally, I thought we had a deal, until the administrator said he had received a phone call from another party and now couldn't complete the deal that night. In other words, the administrator had allowed me to sweat through making a deal just so that he could discern the market price, then let some other party he favoured come in with a slightly better offer and clinch the deal. I left very annoyed, and told him he'd wasted my time; he wouldn't be seeing me again.

The following day at about 6:00 p.m., I got a phone call saying, "Sorry, Mr. Wosskow, would you please come back down here, because the other party's pulled out."

"I don't really want to," I replied. "I said I wasn't going to come back. But now I'm going to come down and make your life a misery."

I had already arranged to have in hand banker's drafts because, when you're buying a company in administration like that, you have to pay right away, with the equivalent of cash. In order to give myself total flexibility in negotiating the price, I had asked for drafts in denominations of £10,000, £25,000, £50,000, £100,000, and £500,000. During the first round of negotiation, before the administrator messed me around, I was acting in good faith, keeping these drafts in my pocket until we'd agreed a fair price. Now, with the deliberate intention of wasting his time like he'd wasted mine, I kept moving these pieces of paper around the table, constantly changing the amount I was offering to pay. I knew I was the sole decent prospect, the only game in town. So I reckoned I could have a little fun at his expense. And I did.

About four in the morning, the administrator slammed his fist down on the desk.

"I am sick and friggin' tired of you and your lawyer and your accountant," he yelled.

He had recently come from doing business with Barings Bank, and he made it clear he was used to dealing with much bigger deals and players than us. Barings Bank was an ancient, oh-so-exclusive, private bank for people with more money than sense. Funnily enough, although none of us knew it that night, venerated Barings was about to go bust in a blaze of scandal, after a twenty-something hotshot broker lost them more than £800 million from illicit investments, practically overnight. "You idiots from Sheffield have been messing me about like this for two days!" the administrator shouted.

"Sorry, sir," I said, a paragon of calm. "But I was always told the moment you've lost your temper is the moment you've lost the argument. You just lost both."

I lowballed him. Hard. He was in a corner, he knew it, and he said yes.

We paid £250,000 for the brand and all the ice cream in storage. They'd estimated the stock of ice cream was worth £150,000, so I was paying £100,000 for the brand. Not a bad deal.

It turned out to be an amazing deal. That administrator may have been used to looking down his nose at people who couldn't afford to bank at Barings, but he didn't know how to perform an accurate stock count. When we took an inventory of all the ice cream in the freezers, there was actually more than £300,000-worth of ice cream. So we bought the whole thing for £250,000, but we actually got it for nothing, because we had £300,000-worth of ice cream we could sell for a profit, and we now had control of the brand, too. Those kinds of deals don't come along very often!

However, as usual, opportunity brought a pressing challenge. We had nowhere to base future production. Bradwell's factory was already getting too small, even for its own output. Loseley was an ice cream company with no way of making ice cream.

As luck would have it, there was another ice cream company in Wales – Snowdonia Ice Cream – which had a gleaming new factory in North Wales with extra capacity. We approached them, and they agreed to make Loseley ice cream for us.

After a while it became clear that their extra capacity was a result of low sales, and they were struggling financially.

So I purchased Snowdonia Ice Cream from another administrator, and the sale brought me that beautiful, spanking new, terrifically modern ice cream factory. Now, we could make ice cream for the Loseley and Snowdonia brands, plus the overflow from Bradwell's in one, custom-made facility. It seemed the future was smooth and sweet. Or so I thought.

The former owner of Snowdonia, who had put his company into administration, was clearly not happy about the situation – despite the fact that we had kindly given him and his family jobs. He got drunk one evening and somehow got access to the factory, after hours. If he couldn't have the factory, no one else could. He punched a hole in a crucial piece of equipment, disabling the generators for the freezers. Unfortunately for him, someone witnessed the whole thing. Fortunately for me, that meant I got a late-night phone call telling me what had happened. Fortunate in the sense that I became aware of the situation almost immediately. But very unfortunate in the sense that I now had to drive from Sheffield to North Wales in the middle of the night while trying to figure out what in the name of choc ice I was going to do with 500,000 litres, or 400,000 lbs, of melting ice cream. Much as I lived for

the thrill of adrenaline that comes from sorting out problems no one's ever dealt with before, my hands were gripping the steering wheel much tighter than I'd have liked as I sped through the miles of gloomily lit motorway.

Somehow, however, if you honestly believe there's a solution to a problem, more often than not, one turns up. Scrambling for options, I remembered Woodward Foodservice, a huge wholesale supplier of food (including frozen) to caterers – located only a few miles from my sabotaged factory, and open 24 hours a day. What were the chances! Now all I had to do was turn on the Wosskow charm.

When you have nearly half a ton of melting ice cream on your hands, charm looks an awful lot like begging. Fortunately, they sympathized with my plight and, with amazing kindness, used their articulated lorries through the night to help move 400 pallets of ice cream from our freezers to theirs.

It was an incredible act of generosity. If they hadn't helped me, it wouldn't have only taken down Snowdonia and Loseley; my whole company would have gone into administration. I told the Woodward's manager at the time that one day I would repay him. I had no idea how I would, only that it was my firm commitment. As I've said before, long-term relationships are incredibly important to the way I choose to do business, and a debt like that needs to be paid when the opportunity presents itself, even if it takes a long time. Sure enough, a few years later, I found myself in a position to award Woodward Foodservice a very substantial contract indeed, to supply Out of Town Restaurants, which you'll read about later.

In the meantime, the vandal ex-owner of Snowdonia Ice cream, who caused all this trouble, had a thoroughly good opportunity to mull the consequences of his own, vastly different, way of doing business, during a hefty jail sentence.

We had the generators mended, took a deep breath, and started making ice cream again.

I was now at the stage where I was talking to the Trafford Centre, near Manchester, about putting in ice cream carts, Free Spirit, and opening the first Speedo shop there, too.

They said, "Lawrence, we'll let you put the ice cream carts in like you did at Meadowhall, but we've got three restaurant units that are unlet. You used to run Café Rouge." That wasn't exactly true, but I went with it. "You know the restaurant business. You've got to take those three restaurants and then we'll let you install the ice cream carts."

I knew the ice cream carts would make a fortune, so I took the three restaurants. Free Spirit was roaring ahead – we had already opened two more stores and signed leases for another eight. With two new ice cream businesses and now Trafford demanding I open three restaurants, I recognized it was too much to handle, so I put Free Spirit up for sale. Millets, the largest outdoor retailer at that time, came in and bought its competitor. I spent time turning Loseley back into a successful ice cream brand with all the lessons learnt from Bradwell's, and then sold it to Thayer's ice cream from South Wales.

That left me free to really concentrate on the three new restaurants in the Trafford Centre, which I incorporated under the name Out of Town Restaurants Ltd. Earlier, I had met Richard Drummond, who ran some restaurants in Meadowhall, while I was trying to sell him ice cream. I approached him now and offered him 10 percent of Out of Town, a good salary and bonuses if he would join my new restaurant business. Even though my offer constituted a cut in pay for him, he jumped at the chance straight away. By September 1998, we had created Bradwell's Sandwiches and Patisseries, Bradwell's English Restaurant, Bitz and Pizzas, and five ice cream carts in the Trafford Centre. Ten percent of the entire population of the UK lives within a 45-minute drive of the Trafford Centre and it currently receives 35 million visits

a year. It took me only a week to realize I could have an incredible business here.

You'd have thought my plate would be full, but then I met a group of great guys from Australia who were launching Bluewater, the fourth-largest shopping centre in the UK, southeast of London, due to open the following March. Since I had loads of knowledge about retail in the UK, I became very useful to them. Once a week, I drove from Sheffield to Bluewater at 4:00 a.m. and returned by 2:00 a.m. the following morning. There was nothing in it for me other than helping them. But it seemed that the more I helped people, the more opportunity came my way.

Sure enough, in December 1998, Bluewater came to me, offering 14 units that remained unlet with only four months until opening. I made it clear that we had no spare money to turn the units into retail spaces, only enough to pay the rent and staff when training began. They were so eager to have us involved, the guys at Bluewater paid millions to set up the units for us, which was completely unheard-of. They let us have all 14 outlets. Then the pressure was really on. We knew what 11 would be, but had no idea about the other three.

Richard Drummond and Steve Gibson, our designer, were tasked with coming up with concepts for all of them. Richard is the guy closest in terms of imagination and creativity to my son Toby, and I admire him so much for his talents, as well as the incredible speed with which he can work. With three outlets as yet completely blank, conceptually, we had a request from Bluewater to meet at the site in two hours. Richard and I got on the train. By the time we arrived at the shopping centre at Blue Water, Richard had designed, named, and drawn pictures of all three outlets. He was a true talent that may never be repeated. He made a lot of mistakes as well, but I learned a lot about being authentic in business from him. Richard always told the truth, no matter how much trouble it got him into. He taught me that if you tell the truth and accept the

blame, you don't ever have to tell any lies. This didn't always make him popular.

For example, at midnight on the night before we were opening the biggest ice cream business in Britain, I looked at Richard and I said, "Where are the cones?"

"Uh, I forgot to order them," he said, all too truthfully.

So I called Jane up in Bradwell, four hours away.

"We haven't got any cones. Can you and Mark get out of bed and drive down to Bluewater with cones?" They were such wonderful people that they made it happen.

Kevin Bracha, who was our centre manager, did an incredible job. I promised him I would give him a huge bonus in a wheelbarrow full of money if he hit certain targets. A few months later, I delivered £5,000 in a wheelbarrow to his office. So somehow or other, with a fantastic team working virtually round the clock, in March 1999, we opened the 14 units in Bluewater, employing 450 people, which immediately made us the largest employer in the centre.

We had now opened the biggest ice cream business and the biggest restaurant business there had ever been in one location. Sales soared, more than doubling almost straight away. We smashed all the goals and budgets we could ever have dreamed of. At Bluewater, we opened Bradwell's Ice Cream, Ben & Jerry's ice cream, Bradwell's English Restaurant, Bradwell's Sandwiches and Patisseries, Fresh Fast Food unit, and a huge Bitz and Pizza with a sports bar upstairs equipped with game machines, and a climbing wall outside. It was insane.

Just a few days after the Bluewater's grand opening, I heard Eddie Healey from Meadowhall was coming for a visit. Since I considered myself to be his protégé, I wanted to show him the astounding amount I'd achieved since he'd given me my big break at Meadowhall, four years earlier. I went looking for him all over Bluewater, and eventually spotted him with his son. He greeted me warmly and agreed to come take a look

at some of our units. I was thrilled to see that he was very proud of what I was doing, but I didn't expect any follow-up, particularly.

However, the next day, I got a phone call from his secretary telling me Eddie wanted to see me at Meadowhall the following morning at 8:00 a.m.

I was aware that he knew only too well that I'd just opened a massive business in Bluewater and should be down there, not in Sheffield. So I knew I was either in trouble or it was important.

I got suited up and went to the meeting. He received me alone, without the large, protective team he normally kept around him.

"If what I am about to tell you now should leave this room, your kneecaps will end up in a different place than where they're supposed to be," he said.

"Mr. Healey," I said, alarmed. "I'm already scared of you. If you tell me something, I'm not going to tell anybody."

He pulled out a thousand-page pile of documents.

"I'm selling Meadowhall for £1.2 billion to British Land," he said.

"I understand confidentiality. Congratulations, you deserve it. You've created several thousand jobs. You've done something for the region and made a big difference in Sheffield," I said.

He then pulled out another stack of documents of about 500 pages. This was a proposal for the sale of the 18 restaurants he owned in Meadowhall to Granada, a huge leisure business in the UK, for £10 million. Until that moment, I had no idea that Eddie owned most of the restaurants in Meadowhall. He'd kept it quiet, putting ownership of them under a company with a different name.

He said he didn't want to sell them to Granada. He wanted me to have them.

He knew I had no ready money, so he'd figured it all out for me. First off, he was going to give me all the businesses, free. The restaurants together had made £1.3 million profit a year for the last three years –

he showed me the books. Therefore, with no investment and simply running the restaurants as they were, I was set to make £1.3 million clear profit. But then, after 12 months, the rent would go up to £1 million a year, leaving me a more modest profit margin. For his part, he could afford to do this because he was getting paid 20 times the rent on the sale of the shopping centre, making the deal worth £20 million to him. It was a dream deal for both of us. Eddie couldn't have imagined how well I would do on his largesse. I almost immediately moved two of the outlets that weren't making any money off onto other operators to do with them as they pleased. With two other units, I halved them in size, which doubled the profits. I changed menus. I raised prices. In some cases, I even changed the whole concept of an outlet. The results were stunning. We made £2 million in profit that first year and, even after the rent went up the following year, we made £1.5 million free and clear.

The deal with Eddie also brought me Simon Heath, someone who became the most influential person in my business life and who is still with me today. I gave Simon 2.5 percent of Out of Town. I was managing director, Richard Drummond was operations director, and Simon was financial director.

What Eddie offered me in his office that day was, in so many ways, an incredible boon. Boons, it turned out, were falling from the sky. We shook hands and I was warned to keep my mouth shut.

The next day, my phone rang again.

"Hi, Lawrence," came a voice I didn't recognize. "It's John Hall." At first, I thought it was John Hall who I grew up with, but I quickly realized it was Sir John Hall, the owner of huge businesses in the northeast, including Newcastle United. He said, "I know you're doing a deal with Eddie Healey."

Of course, I explained I had no idea what he was talking about. But he knew what he knew, and it reflected well on me. I was the guy Eddie Healey trusted to run multiple restaurants in a shopping centre. Sir John owned a great many businesses, and he wanted to sell off 65 food outlets he owned in shopping centres throughout the UK. Some of them were in shopping centres he owned, but not all. I gave him the truth, and told him Out of Town Restaurants had no cash with which to buy new businesses. He didn't care; he wanted a good home for these businesses he had grown. He said £1 was enough. That worked for me. Along with my team at Out of Town, I did all the due diligence and concluded that it was an incredible deal. Another day and another billionaire who was finished playing with a particular toy and wanted to see it taken care of by a trustworthy successor.

For me, this was far from taking on someone else's cast-offs; it was a chance to make my name and my fortune. All in all, during this short period of time, my business – Out of Town Restaurants Group – went from zero turnover to £30 million, and zero staff to 3,000. It was just chaos.

It was 1999 and it was, apparently, raining billionaires who wanted to get rid of businesses. The final ones who called me were the Carphone Warehouse guys. They had invested in a chain of sandwich shops called Ft5K (Feed The 5,000), which were being managed badly and were losing money. Again, £1 did the trick, and it was a perfect acquisition for us. It gave us a recognized sandwich brand name. We sold off the High Street locations, giving us substantial, much-needed cash, and were left with some shopping centre units that made very satisfactory profits indeed.

The real lesson here was to structure things to generate maximum cash flow. The landlords were paying for the fit-outs of the units, so there was no money up front required from me there. Further, I always negotiated 90 days of free rent to start with, sometimes more, so again, no cash required. Meanwhile, suppliers knew they wouldn't get paid for 90 days.

That meant we had three months from the opening of each unit, all of them generating cash income immediately, with the only immediate outflow being wages. Add to that the cash flow coming out of the businesses I'd bought for £1, and cash was pouring in, fueling further expansion.

Getting this whole, complex merry-go-round of interwoven businesses to run smoothly, turning these businesses around, consolidating three head offices into one and goodness knows what else was an absolute mountain of work, really the most stressful period in my life. Those wonderful opportunities that simply fell in my lap, many as a result of building good personal relationships in business, had downsides too – they required a great deal of effort and attention to make them work. I can't say I was immune to the idea of passing some of it onto a worthy buyer.

Within a year, David Coffer, one of the main catering agents in the UK, brought me an offer from Welcome Break – a huge operator of roadside service stations – of £20 million for Out of Town. We were the fastest growing restaurant business the UK had ever seen or was likely to ever see. I told him I'd sell.

But the deal got bogged down and, after seven months, we realized it wasn't going to happen and walked away. It turned out later that the guy at Welcome Break who approached David Coffer never actually had the clearance to buy us out; it was his own dream. There really never was any way for it to happen. But we didn't know that at the time.

By the time the deal fell through, I was so used to running this dizzying whirligig of business operations, I wasn't actually all that bothered. But, sadly, Richard Drummond was, and we lost him. I was very sad, as Richard truly was one of the inspirations behind the business, contributing his creativity to new restaurant designs, names, and operations. After we didn't sell to Welcome Break, he got disheartened. He decided to resign and moved back to Scotland, where he grew up. I had given him 10 percent of the business for free when he signed his contract. If we had sold to Welcome Break for £20 million, he'd have made £2 million. But the contract stated that, in the absence of a sale, if he ever left, I'd get his shares back for nothing.

It seemed too heartbreaking. After all he'd done for the business, I couldn't take it off him for free. So instead, I was very generous with him. He was happy with what I gave him, and so was I. The sale had fallen through and he wanted to leave. Of course, from my perspective, I lost £18 million that would have come in from the deal, and now I was using my own money so that Richard wouldn't go back to Scotland empty-handed. I was very sorry to see him go.

It didn't stop there. Simon Heath heard I'd taken Richard's 10 percent share in the business back and said, "I want that 10 percent." So on top of paying Richard, I then had to turn it over for nothing to Simon Heath, just to keep him in the business. But it was totally worth it. Simon is brilliant with figures, and he's also a tough cookie from whom I've learned a lot. He was the one that carried out functions I always found so difficult, like making people redundant. I always want to be the nice guy, the reasonable guy, the friend, the warm connection. I learned from him that, where you are weak, you need people around you that are stronger than you are. That's probably the most important thing to remember in business – fill the gaps in your skillset with people who are amazing at the things you can't do. Simon and I had a wonderful long-lasting partnership and friendship, and his investment of time, effort and sheer sweat in Out of Town Restaurants deserved a bigger stake in the business.

The failed Welcome Break deal brought another change – it gave me an appetite for selling. So we opened more Out of Town restaurants and spruced everything up, ready for a great offer we were confident would come.

CHAPTER 4

THE KNIGHT RIDES OUT

In late 2002, I was working one hundred hours a week. I was juggling the responsibility of running Out of Town Restaurants, a business with thousands of employees. I was also orchestrating the sale of that business. On top of that, I was putting together an offer to buy another restaurant group – City Centre Restaurants.

As if all that wasn't enough, even when I was running around like a blue-arsed fly, I would get up even earlier in the morning to go to a spinning class. In theory, this was a good idea. I wanted to get all cylinders firing before I started the real work of the day. And if you're working an office job that involves sitting, driving and talking on the telephone, it's wise to stay in shape, of course. But now I know more about how the body works, it's pretty clear that what I was really after was the endorphins delivered into the bloodstream by physical activity. I needed those naturally produced chemicals to help me through what I knew was going to be a very stressful day. There is no doubt in my mind now that I learned to use physical activity to subdue other issues, from a young age and throughout my adult life. I didn't realize it then, of course, but I was fighting a losing battle with stress – taxing my body to deliver drugs that would take the edge off the strains without addressing the root cause. And that, I know now, was a huge amount of underlying anxiety, most likely hereditary. That is why the wheels fell off the bus in the end, as was inevitable. But it took a good long while to get there, as you'll see. First, I decided I was a knight in shining armour and went off on my quests.

City Centre Restaurants included brands like Frankie and Benny's, Garfunkel's, Est Est Est, and Caffe Uno, and it went on to become the Restaurant Group, one of Britain's largest restaurant companies. City Centre was quoted on the full Stock Exchange in London. But the company had gotten quite a bit of bad press lately and wasn't expanding as the boys in The City had hoped it would. Some of the brands were old and tired, and the management was poor. Knowing I had a business that was turning over £30 million, with three thousand employees, making £3 million in profit annually, I set out on a noble mission to rescue it.

The Restaurant Group's biggest brand was Frankie and Benny's, and it was a great example of how to sell food to the British, who are secretly in love with all things American. The outlets style themselves as classic New York and Italian 50s- and 60s-style restaurants, specialising in pizzas, pastas and burgers. The website even relates a soppy story about how Frankie was a poor Sicilian immigrant who landed at New York's Ellis Island in 1924 at the age of ten and helped in the restaurant his poppa opened to highlight his mamma's home cooking. Then, when Poppa retired, Frankie took over the family restaurant with his ol' school pal, Benny. It's like a scene from *The Godfather II*, only the chain was established in Leicester in 1995! If I have learned nothing else about the hospitality business, it is that narrative is what really gets people in the door and then boosts a good experience into one that people seek out again and again. You can have the best food in the world, but unless there's a story behind it, people are not going to come. You can even say a restaurant is an unpretentious hole-in-the-wall that doesn't push itself; that's a story too. People love to discover things.

Despite the appeals of Frankie and Benny's no-doubt heartwarming tale of poor immigrants who offered food like Mamma used to make, the chain was not doing well, and the management wanted to buy the business. It made sense to me that, once that happened, the group would be broken up, and I set up the deals accordingly. I agreed to sell Frankie and Benny's to their management, Est Est Est to another restaurant business, Cafe Uno to a private equity house, and Chiquito Restaurant Bar and Mexican Grill to their own management, too. The way the arithmetic worked out, with the price of the shares I was paying the owners set against the money I'd receive from the various buyers, I would basically end up with Garfunkel's for free after the break-up. In those days, Garfunkel's profit was £8 million a year, net, and it was worth £100 million.

It sounds dreamy as a big pepperoni pizza pie, but there was a snag – I needed to raise a lot of capital personally in order to buy City Centre. In order to do that, I had to complete the sale of Out of Town Restaurants. City Centre was ready to go. Like most publicly quoted companies, there were tens of thousands of shareholders, but two institutions owned 20 percent of the business, so they really controlled how the sale would go down, if at all. Knowing my interest, those two institutions got in touch with me to sell me their shares, and we agreed on a deal. Unfortunately, this happened before I could complete the sale of Out of Town Restaurants, so there was a delay in pushing it through.

The delay ended up being disastrous. While I was waiting for capital to be freed up from the sale of Out of Town, the management of City Centre Restaurants Group brought in a new chairman who was experienced in the restaurant business. He convinced the main shareholders not to do the deal they'd agreed to with me, but instead give him and the people he brought in a chance to turn things around. If I had gotten the cash in time, they would have been happy to push the sale through, but by the time I sold Out of Town Restaurants, it was too late.

All this really added to the stress I was feeling in the three months leading up to the sale, which was a very hectic time. When you're selling a business of that size, there's a bidding process and then the buyer has to do due diligence, which is intrusive, complex and tiresome. For myriad reasons, there's a lot of time spent with lawyers and accountants. Plus, don't forget, you have to keep the business running in the meantime, and running well. You don't want it to suddenly tank while the deal is unsigned! In any case, there were a lot of moving parts. Despite the size and complexity of Out of Town and the deal we were putting together, I had kept our team very lean. It consisted of Simon Heath as managing director, and just one lawyer, Trevor Ironmonger. Trevor was a local lawyer from Sheffield, with whom I'd done every deal since the day I started, because I trusted him absolutely. Together with me, that made a total of three.

I can't tell you how hilarious it was to walk into meetings with the people who were buying Out of Town – these were almost always in London – and be ushered into some high-ceilinged room in an imposing office, through to one end of a vast conference table where we faced a team of at least twelve lawyers, plus different people from the private equity houses. I laugh when I look back on those meetings and think about Simon, Trevor, and me sitting at one end of the table against the 15 to 20 people at the other end.

With so many people involved, I suppose I shouldn't have been surprised when the final leg of the deal turned out to be sheer torture. We spent the whole week in London, on tenterhooks. First the deal was on, then off, then on, then off again, hampered by one complication after another until the very end. The private equity house approached Simon Heath on the side and suggested lowering the price, but Simon warned them not to try that, because he knew me well enough to believe that I would walk away, which was completely correct.

The shenanigans back and forth had me pretty annoyed as it was. I had threatened to leave on the last train back to Sheffield on Friday night whether the deal was completed or not. I'm sure they thought I was bluffing. The deal was supposed to be completely done on Thursday night, and then a further complication was found at 3:00 a.m. That took us into Friday morning. The buyer's team promised the deal would be wrapped by no later than noon, but it wasn't. When I left the lawyers' office in London at 9:00 p.m., it was still not complete. I hadn't seen my children and my wife for a week, and I'm a man of my word, so I made good on my promise. I took a taxi to the station. Simon Heath stayed behind.

I got to St. Pancras at 10:15 to catch the last train back to Sheffield at 10:30 p.m., but I was still hopeful. I rang Simon Heath from the station and asked, "Is the deal complete?"

Simon sighed heavily. "Lawrence," he said. "There have been further problems." My heart sank.

But then, in the background, I heard champagne corks popping. The deal was complete; he was only joking! I was overcome by euphoria. After all that had happened during the last three months and that long, long week, I broke down in tears, releasing all the pressure that had been building up. By the time I got back to Sheffield, it was about one o'clock in the morning. Julie came down to the station to pick me up and we just hugged for some time, in shared relief.

I'm not sure how many entrepreneurs cry over business deals – especially ones that go through successfully. Maybe it's a common thing. But some part of me knew I was burning myself out to the core. I wasn't completely unaware of the need to slow down. Throughout the sales process, I made it very clear that I wouldn't stay behind with the business. Most buyers want the previous owner to stay behind for at least a year or two to ensure a smooth transition before fully handing it over. But that was why it was smart to make sure Simon Heath had 10 percent of the business. It meant not only that he was always committed, but also that he could be the one who stayed behind and handed over the business. And that, indeed, is what he did when I left. As a result, the morning after the deal went through, I had sold Out of Town, but I hadn't bought City Centre Restaurants. Contrary to plans, therefore, and somewhat to my astonishment, I woke up a free man.

The first thing I did was book a trip for Hannah, Toby, Julie, and me on Concorde to New York. The primary purpose of the trip was to celebrate, but it also conveniently took me away from the British press, who were very interested in the deal I'd just done. From the beginning of my career, I'd attracted media coverage. The Bradwell's purchase was a good example – I was characterized as a young *impresario* who'd made good in London and came back to his hometown to take over a sleepy little ice cream company. It was a tale of North and South, of tradition bowing to audacious new ideas, all with a touch of "who does he think he is?" class-tension thrown in – a compelling story, in other words, about worlds colliding. Over the following years, I learned to use the press well to help me launch products (Nora Batty was the first of many arresting ideas) and generally getting good publicity for my businesses. That was all great while I was building them but, having sold up, I was exhausted and in need of peace and quiet. Media attention was the last thing I wanted. So I did what any subject of unwanted media attention would do – I skipped the country.

On Sunday morning, we made our escape. It was the first time we'd flown on Concorde, which was amazing. It was cramped, of course, but the service was incredible and, because of the time difference, you got from London to New York so fast, you arrived before you'd started! It's so sad to think that, less than a year later, Concorde was mothballed forever. Richard Branson tried to buy the planes from British Airways, but of course his old rivals wouldn't come to the table with him. I'm delighted to hear that Club Concorde has now received funding to revive supersonic travel.

We stayed at the Four Seasons Hotel in Manhattan, which was designed by I.M. Pei, the architect who put the glass pyramid on the Louvre, among other spectacular modern structures. The penthouse suite rents out for $50,000 a night, making it one of the most expensive hotel suites in the world. We didn't take the penthouse, but we did have an incredible, luxurious few days there. My attempt to duck media attention worked; it was funny to see all the headlines and newspaper articles about the sale in the UK from a safe distance.

One chance encounter during the trip that really stands out for me was a brush with Richard Wolf, the owner of a restaurant called Tao. The first evening we were in town, we asked the concierge what the new trendy, hip restaurant was in our neighborhood. He recommended Tao and got us a reservation there. I'd never seen anything like it. Originally a 19th century stable for the Vanderbilt family and then a balconied movie theater, the space had been transformed by Wolf and his team into a majestic Asian "temple". We were awestruck by the giant gold 16-foot-tall Buddha that seems to float over a reflecting pool complete with Japanese carp, and the buzz of 300 people eating on three different levels. New York restaurants take that narrative element I was talking about to a whole new level – it's more like theatre plus food – an experience for all the senses. We loved it.

Because we were celebrating, I ordered a bottle of Cristal champagne. Then I ordered another. That's when Richard Wolf approached our table. He asked, "Are you celebrating? Because it's not often that people come in here and order two bottles of Cristal." I explained that I'd just sold my business in the UK and we'd flown over on Concorde and, yes indeed, we were celebrating.

His response truly took me aback. Here he was, owner of one of the hottest restaurants in New York, in the flux, master of this amazing space and vibe, and what he said was, "All I dream of is being like you one day." He didn't say it in an envious way. He just knew what he wanted.

I never saw him again, but I do know that he achieved his dream, and a great deal more. Now, he could probably buy me out ten times over. He has the busiest restaurant/nightclub in the world in Las Vegas, selling over a million dollars a week, and many other incredibly successful restaurants, bars and nightclubs all over the US and in Australia, with his partners at Tao Group.

Another incident that was to take on greater significance was a visit to the wonderful New York institution called Hammacher Schlemmer, which was full of amazing modern toys and books. I picked up a book called *101 Things to Do Before You Die*, which I started to read on the plane back. Some of it – like collecting stamps – simply didn't appeal and didn't feel relevant to me, but it got me thinking. I began to think about what I would do for the foreseeable future. All my time and energy before we sold Out of Town, all the way back, if I was honest, was focused on either buying the next business or selling and running the business that I had. There had never been any time to think what I was going to do next. I also thought about what had brought me to this stage of my life. I started formulating my own list of 101 things I wanted to do before I died. In honor of my roots as a Sheffield guy, I called it "The Full Monty, 101 Things to Do Before I Die."

If you haven't seen the film *The Full Monty*, or it's been a long time, I thoroughly recommend that you watch it. On the surface, it's a heartwarming, quirky comedy about a group of unemployed mates who get together to raise money for the lead character's child support by putting on a Chippendales-style strip show. Only, because they're a bunch of ordinary, local lads, they need to add an extra element to attract the desired crowd, so they decide they'll strip off totally naked – the "Full Monty" of the title. On a deeper level, however, it's actually about some much more serious issues, not least among them the emasculating effect of economic stultification and the way it plays out between fathers and sons, husbands and wives. Set against a backdrop of Sheffield in the late 90s, it shows the devastating effect on a once-vibrant community that was economically sustained by a single industry (in this case, steel) when that single industry goes bust. I know about all of these things first-hand. I grew up in an atmosphere of decline that was as inevitable as gravity. The simple laws of supply and demand were pulling everything and everyone down, down, down. Into poverty. Into drunkenness and drug addiction and violence. Into themselves. Into anger and resentment.

It wasn't all bad, of course; one of the things I love about the film is that it shows how strong and independent and funny the people of Sheffield are. But in many ways, my family was a microcosm of what was going on.

In my early years, I was quiet and gentle. But my parents had a difficult marriage. My mum was a soft, loving woman with mental health issues, and my dad was a hardened businessman, making my home, a difficult place to live in. My parents finally split when I was eight and my sister, Karen, was nine.

Mum, who had always suffered from anxiety and mental health issues, ended up in a mental institution for periods of time. After she was released, she was prescribed Benzodiazepines. Like many psychoactive pharmaceuticals, this class of drug works to increase the brain's ability to absorb a chemical it produces naturally, compensating for the fact that the brain is not taking up enough of it as a neurotransmitter – in this case, gamma-aminobutyric acid (GABA). Too little GABA absorption, and you become anxious and over-excited, which was her tendency. Too much GABA in the system, however, and you can end up in a coma. Doctors at the time didn't realize how dangerous these drugs were, nor how addictive. Twice, at 10 and 11 years old, I had to call an ambulance when I found Mum lying insensible on the couch, overdosed on these prescription drugs.

All the while, deep inside, I was desperately looking for stability and love, and I think that's why I was ready for a fully committed relationship at 17. Thank goodness it was with Julie. With her, I was able to find a loving, safe partner for life. I was scared to get married, true, because of what had happened with my mum and dad, but I took the plunge anyway because I longed for a stable home life, with children who were being brought up in a solid family unit with lot of love and laughter. I have been incredibly fortunate to achieve that. But the underlying problems from my childhood dogged me for many more years than I was willing to admit for a long time.

Before Julie, my life was very volatile. Because of my disruptive behavior at school, I was asked to leave my junior school a year early. At my new school, still misbehaving, I was put in the bottom class. Things got worse as I got involved with the wrong crowd and spiraled out of control. I had a number of brushes with the police, and it wasn't long before I realized that I needed an outlet for my internal anger.

Eventually, I started doing things that made my life better, that gave me the endorphins in a healthy way – football, tennis and table-tennis, in which I got good enough to represent my school. But I never quite reached my potential in those sports because there was always something niggling me and distracting me: a party or a girl. The only end-of-year school report of which I was ever proud was when my headmaster commented, "If Lawrence put as much effort into his work as he did the girls, he'd be a genius."

Fanaticism was a way of life for me at that age. I joined up with the hooligan element of Sheffield United, my cherished football team. For the next few years, I travelled to 90 out of 92 league grounds, as we went from Division 1 to Division 4 and back up again in triumph. I was supporting my team, of course, but I was also exhilarated by what went along with the sport – the violence.

This was the golden age of football violence, before knives and clubs and even guns made it an undeniably criminal scourge that had to be policed tightly and preferably eradicated entirely. Football was, and always will be, a working man's game. It's the Beautiful Game, but not beautiful like something you'd put in an art gallery where people shush you if you talk too loud. It's the astonishing beauty that happens when 22 really skilled players kick a ball around for 90 minutes. It's endlessly complex and simple, full of intricate moves and big, bold kicks, hope and despair, drama and disappointment, goals and near misses. And loyalty. This was before players changed teams and countries like they got new sports cars, with tens of millions of pounds changing hands, driving ticket prices through the roof. This was when the cheap seats anyone could afford weren't seats at all but terraces – broad steps of concrete where you stood, crushed and jostling among a mass of fans who were swilling lager and yelling like animals and you'd better not wear a coat with pockets because you might well find them full of urine next time you put your hand in there. This was a different era than the one we live in now, when George Best – the finest dribbler that ever lived – could get away with being a drunk who beat his girlfriends, and Peter Shilton got off with a £350 fine and 15-month driving ban for crashing into a lamppost, drunk, at 5 a.m. in a country lane, trying to escape the husband of the partially clothed woman in his car. It was the age of nodding and winking at "laddish" behavior, when a good, lager-fuelled fight on a Saturday night was regarded by many as letting young men blow off some steam. And that applied to "rows" between football "firms", in the days before they became militarized war games with regular fatalities. Your life was rarely in danger at a football match but, if you weren't interested in risking a burst lip, you'd better know how to steer clear of the mob, and avoid standing out or looking vulnerable.

I had no intention of steering clear. I was looking for trouble, and I managed to find plenty of it.

For me, those days were incredible. The sense of being part of a team – always backing each other up, even when the odds were stacked against you – led to great friendships. There were too many close encounters to mention, but one that stands out was when Sheffield United played Chelsea in London.

Most of the Sheffield United hooligan element, known as the Blades Business Crew, met up, in the World's End Pub in Camden. What we didn't know then was that our sworn enemy, Sheffield Wednesday, had been in touch with Chelsea's gangs to tell them where we were. Chelsea's bovver boys came marching down the street, fully armed with bricks, bottles, and even a machete. We were in the hundreds; the police were completely outnumbered and could do nothing at all. A string of serious fighting began, which was reminiscent of another film – *Green Street*.

I loved it all. The danger. The battle cries. The sense of being with fellow men in a tight group, standing against another group of tightly loyal fellow men. The onset of chaotic violence, when the outcome is far from clear. The absolute focus on the moment, to the exclusion of any other consideration, any other thought.

The risk. The adrenaline. The rush.

I needed it.

And, now, years later and even at a crucial stage where I could have left all the stress behind, that need for a rush was coming closer and closer to killing me.

In hindsight, my advice to others is not to suddenly quit if you've been running your engine at maximum capacity consistently for years. I've advised athletes who retire and asked, "How can you go from your body expecting the adrenaline of doing what you've done for the last 25 years, non-stop, to suddenly stopping? How do you expect your body and your mind to react?"

Similarly, my advice to any businessperson is: "Do not go at it 100 miles an hour for 25 years and then suddenly stop, because it's dangerous. It sounds great, but it's not very clever."

What a shame someone wasn't around to give me the same advice in 2002. I stopped cold because I didn't know any better. I didn't know anyone who had done it the right way – or a different way, at least – to advise me.

What I'd done with those few days in New York was calm down and take a breath after the sale. I'd thought of something to do for the foreseeable future – not forever – to be able to replace the adrenaline, fear and the excitement of running businesses, something different to business. And whereas most people I know replace business with business and go on to the next takeover, the next challenge to boost profits and raise revenue, I was choosing a different path.

Some people tell me, "I absolutely love what I do." I never quite got to that stage. I never woke up and thought, "I can't wait to get to the office. I can't wait to get to the restaurant. I can't wait to get to work. I'm really looking forward to it." I enjoyed moments when we were striking deals very much, even though I found it extremely stressful. I discovered, early on, when M&S sent me on a course on negotiating skills, that I was good at brokering deals – very good. Sometimes, I think it's really the only thing I'm good at. It comes naturally to me:

When I'm talking to the cleaner, I'm a cleaner. I'm a football hooligan when I'm with one, and I'm a chief executive when I'm with that person. My real skill, which I never learned in a formal way, is that I mirror the person I am talking to. That, in turn, puts them at their ease in deep ways psychologists are only really beginning to understand now – something called "mirror neurons" that make your mouth water when you see someone eat something on the TV. I've always enjoyed the cut and thrust of buying and selling, for sure. But negotiating is what really makes my heart sing.

Most business people who I've met are scared to do something different. They love what they do, they're good at it, and they get into the comfort zone of doing deals, and carry on doing them. A lot of them feel that more is always better. But I realized, I had "more". Now that I had enough money set aside in the bank to do whatever I wanted, and the security of knowing that, I started figuring out what it was that I really wanted to do. When writing down my list of 101 things, I thought about my dreams and what I personally enjoyed doing, and tried to tie them together.

One of the things I had always loved doing was to travel. So Nidge, Tim and I set off to Brazil on a trip to Rio de Janeiro, the jungles of the Amazon, and then to Machu Picchu in Peru, all on my tab. It was such an amazing luxury to be able to kick back and enjoy life with my two best mates, travelling First Class all the way, on the fruits of my labours. My visit to Machu Picchu, however, delivered a message about work and leisure that I misinterpreted at the time.

We flew from Rio to Lima and then from Lima to Cuzco, which is where the base sets off to go to Machu Picchu. The flight takes you from zero altitude to about twelve thousand feet or more in only 80 minutes. When we got there, the owner of the guest house where we were staying gave us tea made from coca leaves. That's the plant used to make cocaine, but with a great deal of chemical intervention, so this form was presented as pretty benign. Coca tea is supposed to help with altitude sickness. It certainly didn't help me.

That evening, I couldn't slow my heart down and I was getting terrible headaches. In the middle of the night, I called a taxi to drive me to as low an altitude as possible, which was still about ten thousand feet, and slept down there. The next day, all my motor neuron usages of my hands, feet, and legs felt different. I wasn't able to walk. Tim came down that afternoon and took me to the local hospital, where nobody spoke English. The symptoms got worse and worse, culminating in me receiving oxygen for a period of about 24 hours.

Tim had taken the same tea and was absolutely fine, just heartbroken that we couldn't get up to Machu Picchu. Together, we all made the decision to get out of there, and booked a flight. Cuzco, the only place we could fly out of, was actually at a higher altitude, so I had to use the oxygen cylinder to go back up, but I made it okay. We flew back to Brazil, and made frequent trips to hospital, as I was still feeling the effects of whatever had happened.

For some reason that neither I nor my doctors can identify, the event took a serious toll on me. It was the first stage of the life-changing shift in my body. When I came back to the UK, I started waking up at night with panic attacks. I ended up in and out of the hospital because I couldn't slow my heart rate down.

Without meaning to, I suddenly found myself stuck at home feeling ill, with nowhere to go. It was as if something was stuck inside my body, running round and round and round, and then going into my head making me dizzy, making my heart beat fast. There was no outlet for it. It was like living in an adrenaline world.

The symptoms got worse and worse and the doctors took more and more blood tests; nobody could find anything wrong with me. One day, I was talking to a guy called David, who used to work as my driver sometimes and had suffered similar symptoms. He told me that he had problems early on in his life and that he believed what happened to him was mental and not physical. He was the first person to say that.

When I started investigating deeply into what this could mean, I found that mental healthcare in the UK was a complete disaster. There was no budget and nobody who really understood these issues. My symptoms spiraled further and further out of control over the next year. I looked into the research – particularly in Finland, of all places – and they have found that anxiety is hereditary. I realized I had something that was out of my control. I thought that it *should* be in my control, but it wasn't.

As I've told you, my mother had suffered terribly with anxiety her whole life. I watched her pour drugs down her throat; in fact, I had to give them to her when I was a young kid, and at that early age, I had decided I was not going to take any drugs. That was my initial and my long-term strategy. In hindsight, it was a mistake. In later years, I did take some drugs. But at this time, the only pills offered to me were the same GABA-enhancing drugs my mom had taken so disastrously.

There was no way I was going to become addicted to those drugs. The new type of drugs that they were experimenting with hadn't been proven over a long period. They were also geared towards depression rather than anxiety, though researchers later found out those drugs do also have some impact on anxiety. Those particular drugs were not confidently recommended to me by my doctors, however, so I remained cautious. Perhaps if they'd told me, "This is exactly what you need," I'd have been more open to the intended effect. I think a lot of mental health care is about believing in what is offered, rather than the actual clinical efficacy of the drugs, but that's just my opinion.

In any case, I was left to figure out an alternative to drugs. I found a guy in Sheffield – which had hardly any facilities for mental health – who offered Cognitive Behavioral Therapy. CBT is a talk therapy that focuses on exploring and identifying patterns of thoughts, feelings and behaviors. It's generally pretty finite, delivering at least some results quickly, because after you've worked to uncover unhealthy patterns of thought and how they may be causing self-destructive behaviors and beliefs, you address the behaviors, not the underlying causes. Its appeal for many is that you're not lying on a couch for months talking about your mother, but instead catching yourself every time you start to get into a mental whirlpool.

The CBT treatment helped a bit, but one of the main things the therapist asked was, "Lawrence, when all these symptoms are happening, what is it you're terrified of? What's the worst thing that can happen?"

I realized that, in a completely counter-intuitive way, my fear was of my heart slowing down and coming back to normal. Because then I'd have to face the underlying anxiety that I inherited from my mother and that had plagued me, progressively, all my life. All the years I'd been running at 100 miles an hour, I had used stress to keep the anxiety below the surface. I'd been too busy for it to ever come out. But when illness forced me to slow down and do nothing, it came out – big time. When I look back, I believe it was a miracle that I managed to keep it repressed for so long. Really, it was just a matter of time before it came out. Maybe it was the total cessation of business-related freneticism that brought it out; maybe it was the altitude sickness in Peru. Whatever the cause, it became truly debilitating.

I remember my best friend Nidge saying to me, "Lawrence, you know, you've been through so many things. This is not like you; what's happening?"

I said to him, "To be honest, Nigel, I would prefer to fall off a building and break every bone in my body than go through what I'm going through now because I know that they will heal eventually; I don't know that this will."

As my symptoms became intolerable, I turned back to the only thing I knew for sure that had worked in the past – a business challenge.

I felt driven to throw myself back into something to be able to keep busy and push this all back down beneath the surface. The timing was perfect. My nadir occurred two years after the sale; Simon Heath had finished handing over Out of Town Restaurants to the buyers and was available for a new project.

With fateful timing, this was exactly when Little Chef became available. I saw a chance of getting deeply involved with an iconic brand that I'd always wanted to manage, turn it around, and bring it back to its past glory. I jumped at the opportunity, not only because it was what I'd always dreamt of doing, but because it offered me a chance to make myself "better" by getting busy again.

Little Chef became the killer deal in more than one way. But in a sense, it was also my savior, because it allowed me to ramp up my crazy anxiety-cloaking energies to the point where my body simply couldn't take it anymore. The cure was worse than the disease. So when I look back on it now, I realize that Little Chef probably saved my life. Although, of course, by the same token, it nearly ended it.

CHAPTER 5

LITTLE CHEF: AN ICONIC BRAND

I'm not the first person to have observed that many great business ideas originate in America, nor am I unique in observing that Brits secretly covet the American way of life, at least as they imagine it. But it is worth remembering these facts, because Little Chef – established in 1958 by London-born caravan designer and manufacturer Sam Alper – brilliantly encapsulated both of them. Roadside eateries, positioned to offer weary travelers sustenance while minimizing the delay in continuing their journeys, have been going since the Silk Route and earlier, no doubt. But America truly brought the concept of roadside dining to a new level in the 1950s. The magic ingredient was a consistent, reliable eating experience.

Anyone who drove long distances across America before McDonald's and other fast-food chains began their spread into every corner of the country will tell you that, for every heartwarmingly well-run family diner offering delicious homemade food served with a friendly smile, there were ten dismal establishments slinging inedible gristle and grease (with a dose of *E. coli* thrown in with alarming regularity). Furthermore, from the road, it was almost impossible for travelers to distinguish between these establishments, or to know that there was a less foul-smelling place just a couple of miles down the road. When Ray Kroc began franchising the McDonald brothers' pared-down, fast-food menu across the nation, including by the side of America's highways, he brought an element of predictability and reliability that simply had never been on offer from restaurants before. Before feedlots and "pink slime" and super-sizing and skyrocketing childhood obesity and all the other controversies that hamper the public's relationship with fast food, the McDonald's proposition was, arguably, a purely positive one. If you saw the golden arches, you knew you were going to get a decent meal. You even knew what your menu options would be, and could anticipate a cheeseburger that was pretty much exactly the same as the one you had last time. This was a huge, game-changing development in the world of food retail and it continues to reverberate today.

It was exactly that phenomenon Sam Alper and catering veteran Peter Merchant recognized and decided to bring to the British public. Wimpy, which opened its first restaurant in 1954 in London in conjunction with Lyons (purveyor of wildly popular tea shops since 1894), quickly took over the market for reliable-quality food, served quickly, within the towns and inner-city locations in Britain. But Alper's stroke of genius was identifying the extra appeal for fast, predictable food to travelers. He also correctly recognized the changes taking place in people's driving habits because of the rapidly growing network of faster "A" roads built after World War II, which were designed for speedy, cross-country driving. Britain, more than ever, was on the move. And it was hungry.

So it was also ripe for the concept that Alper and Merchant brought back from a business trip to America. They decided to open an 11-seat diner caravan on Oxford Road in Reading, named "Little Chef", after the American diner that had inspired him. At the time, transport cafés mostly served lorry drivers and bikers; Alper designed his restaurant to cater to families, an underserved market.

The first Little Chefs had basic, prefabricated construction. Three or four staff members served no more than twenty customers. The menu consisted of traditional British fare, with all-day breakfast items, burgers, grills, steaks, haddock or cod, which were all served with chips.

By 1965, there were 12 Little Chefs, with newer models built from brick, offering tables for forty customers. They standardized their décor and uniforms and trained staff. Three years later, with 25 Little Chefs across the UK, Alper sold portions of the company to Merchant, who developed the concept through his Merchant Group. They later merged with John Gardner Catering and formed Gardner Merchant, which became a subsidiary of Trust Houses in 1968.

As the company expanded, newer restaurants were built with room for 60 customers, more parking, consistent sign boards and other branding efforts. There were 44 Little Chef restaurants when Trust Houses merged with Charles Forte's hotel and catering empire and became Trust House Forte in 1970, when I was seven years old and already enjoying their chips. The takeover provided enough funding to help Little Chef expand even more quickly.

Planning permission, however, was a problem. So Forte approached well-located transport cafes and paid owners huge sums of money to sell and move out within a week so the cafes could be converted into Little Chefs. This resulted in the chain expanding to 100 Little Chefs by

1972, mostly self-service. By 1976, there were 174 restaurants between Aberdeen and Plymouth. In 1976, the first Little Chef Lodge, offering a place for overnight stopovers, opened in Scotland; more stopovers were added throughout the decade. The famous Jubilee Pancakes were added to the menu in 1977.

By the 1980s, the chain was dispersed throughout the country, with its prominent red and white "Fat Charlie" logo acting as a guiding light for everyone from hungry families to traveling businessmen. Throughout the decade, Little Chef outlets opened at larger Trust House Forte service areas on motorways and trunk roads. The company, now Welcome Break, bought the Happy Eater roadside restaurant chain, Little Chef's prime competitor at the time, in 1986, later mothballing the brand.

Little Chef Lodges continued to open throughout the country until 1990, when they were rebranded as Travelodge after Forte's acquisition. Pasta and salads were introduced to the menu in the early 1990s. In 1994, the iconic Olympic Breakfast was added.

Forte developed a spin-off takeaway operation brand called "Little Chef Express" in 1995 to compete with fast food outlets in shopping centres and airport terminals. Only five of these restaurants were built on the roadside, and the idea was redeveloped when Little Chef was taken over by Compass, with the Express takeouts established in food courts, including one in the Eurostar terminal.

In 1996, Granada, the catering and broadcasting conglomerate, mounted a successful takeover of the Forte group, and Sam Alper sold his final stake in the company. Granada closed the Little Chef coffee stops, adapting most of them to Burger King outlets.

Granada sold the Welcome Break chain, and the Little Chefs at those motorway service areas became Red Hen, another table service restaurant. In 1998, Granada bought AJ's Family Restaurants, another

Little Chef rival, from the Celebrated Group, and converted all of its 15 sites to Little Chefs.

At the turn of the millennium, the numbers peaked, with 439 restaurants. Most of the restaurants were located on sites on A-roads, often paired with a Travelodge motel and a petrol station. In 2000, Granada merged with the Compass Group to form Granada Compass, but the two demerged in 2001 leaving Little Chef as part of Compass.

In 2002, Permira, a private equity business, bought Travelodge and Little Chef from Compass Group for £712 million. They created a special purpose vehicle called TLLC Group Holdings, specifically to own and manage Little Chef.

After the peak in 2000, the march towards decline began. High prices earned Little Chef the nickname "Little Thief." Some blamed owners, from Granada onwards, for extracting money from the business without investing in updating it. Another challenge was the rise of restaurants in pubs, which were changing to cater to both businesses and families.

In 2005, Travelodge announced that 130 underperforming restaurants would close, shrinking the chain to 234 restaurants. Little Chef and Travelodge in Ireland were sold off to new operators and the Little Chefs rebranded. In the years leading up to 2005, Granada had been gradually reducing the number of restaurants. That year, Travelodge Hotels Ltd. declared their plans to sell the chain.

And that's the convoluted story of how it came to me.

How I came to it, on the other hand, is fairly simple.

Little Chef had a very special place in my childhood. Throughout the 70s, my mum, sister, grandparents and I took our annual family holiday in Bournemouth on the South Coast. In those days, it was far more pleasant to stay off the motorways and take "trunk", A roads, and the journey took between nine and ten hours each way. We ate breakfast, lunch and dinner at Little Chef, always leaving with a full tummy and a lollipop. Hearing that Little Chef was up for sale triggered the same feelings of nostalgia that I'd had, years earlier, for Bradwell's ice cream.

For me, the main attraction of Little Chef was reflecting on so many happy memories with my family. I knew I wasn't the only one who felt this way; everybody from the road sweeper to the prime minister thought fondly about spending time at this iconic establishment. But, while Little Chef lived on in the memories of millions of people, those memories were beginning to sour. The brand was declining rapidly, now becoming famous for poor-quality food, high pricing, and the run-down state of the buildings. What was acceptable in the austere, post-rationing 60s and 70s was now dowdy and outdated.

So that's when Simon Heath and I came into the picture. We heard that Little Chef was up for sale just as Simon was about to finish handing over Out of Town Restaurants to the buyer. I was struggling with my health and still committed to buying an iconic brand. It was a golden opportunity, so we said, "Let's try to do it."

One of the hard-to-quantify elements that influenced my decision to go for it was that there was an extraordinary, sentimental persistence of the vision of what Little Chef should be in the British imagination. In 2001, the Compass Group tried to introduce meals by Harry Ramsden, which they owned, in a cross-branding exercise. In theory, adding fast-food fish and chips to Little Chef's menu and image made sense – the clientele was remarkably similar. However, the public roundly rejected it and the brand was withdrawn.

Another failed attempt to modernize Little Chef's image happened just before the opportunity arose for me to buy it. In August 2004, Little Chef's chief executive Tim Scoble announced plans to change the logo to a slimmer version of Fat Charlie, the chain's mascot. Scoble said Little Chef's management was getting complaints from the public about Fat Charlie being, well… fat. Others said that Fat Charlie was, in fact, a small child, who should not be carrying hot food, as it was dangerous. A new logo was unveiled. Honestly, you can Google it. It wasn't even that radical – they just slimmed down his waistline a bit. But, oh my goodness, people hated it! Some 15,000 customers actually took the trouble to complain. The evidence was undeniable; there was something deep and enduring in the Little Chef brand, if only someone could identify, honour and nurture it. I believed in my heart that people would prefer breaking their journey at Little Chef over Starbucks if changes were made to modernize the cherished institution and make it more appealing. I decided that was my mission.

It helped, of course, that this was yet another Mission: Almost Impossible.

Simon and I both knew it was going to cost a lot of money to buy Little Chef, and we didn't know where we would find that much money, but we went down to London to make a bid anyway. When we presented ourselves to the Travelodge board, we knew we were competing against some of the biggest private equity houses in England. Before we got there, during, and after the meeting, we could tell that we were low on the list of buyers. It seemed fair enough – the other bidders already had all the money they needed to make the purchase, and we didn't. Travelodge knew that perfectly well. They were dealing with some serious players. It was hard to put us in the same category, frankly. But we gave it our best shot.

After the meeting was over, Simon and I came out a bit downtrodden. Normally, we'd have gone for a meal somewhere nice, but in our rather subdued state of mind, we decided to instead just grab a sandwich at the cafe opposite Travelodge's head office. Minutes after we sat down, the CEO of Travelodge, to whom we had just been presenting half an hour earlier, walked in with his daughter. I invited them to join us at our table, and offered to buy them lunch. As we got to chatting, I found out that his daughter was going backpacking. Now, this was an area where I could go toe-to-toe with the best of them! I spent the next 45 minutes telling her about where to go, what to do, and what not to do. She was really engaged, even taking careful notes. I honestly offered it in the spirit of passing forward the kindnesses I had from fellow travelers all over the world, without thinking of any payback. But, of course, her father witnessed the whole thing – including not only my enthusiasm and adventurous nature, but my genuine concern. He had been worried about his nearest and dearest going off on her own. Now, he was sending her on her way with some sound advice. He was very grateful.

I may be generous, but I wasn't going to let an advantage like that go to waste. At the end of our lunch, I took the opportunity to broach the subject of the impending deal. I pointed out to the CEO that, while there might be many larger companies bidding on Little Chef, since I had made up my mind to put in £5 million, I was the only person who was willing to put up his own money. All the other bidders, I observed, were using other people's money. So I argued he shouldn't just be looking at financial strength when he made this decision. He should be asking himself whom he could work with, whom he trusted, and who was 100 percent committed to making this venture succeed. Further, since a lot of Little Chef sites were on the same sites as Travelodge – some of them actually inside them – we were effectively going to be partners, working very closely together. Travelodge would have a hard time protecting its image if Little Chef didn't improve, and fast.

I'm not honestly sure what it was – the presentation, my convincing words at lunch or my travel tips – but we ended up becoming the chosen party. It was fantastic news, and Simon and I rejoiced for a good five minutes before asking ourselves where on earth we were going to get the £60 million we'd agreed with Travelodge. At this stage, we didn't know how much money we could borrow from the bank against the Little Chef business. So the first thing we did was get the restaurant properties valued by CBRE, the world's largest valuer. That evaluation came in at

While I traveled across the Little Chef Empire visiting these sites, Simon Heath was back at the office, looking through all the financial data that had been provided by Permira. He found a number of holes. In all these business deals, numbers can be read to say whatever you want them to say. Simon was reading them one way; they were reading them another. We knew that Permira was a very large company, and that its main focus was Travelodge. Little Chef was a sideshow for them. We also knew about the line-up of buyers that they had had on hold because of us, and that we were number one at this stage.

After performing all this due diligence, we were the sole buyers, which is normal in the due diligence period. We therefore knew that the other potential buyers had probably disappeared by now. With the holes in the numbers exposed, we determined that we weren't going to pay £60 million – the amount that we bid to become the sole buyer.

We had to decide, in that case, what we were willing to pay, what Permira would accept, and at what number we could meet to make it worthwhile for both parties. We'd already spent £1.2 million on lawyers, accountants, evaluations and everything the banks required. They had probably spent £1 million as well. So we were both wedded to each other. They had – probably mistakenly – already announced the sale to the press. So this was a big deal; it was featured in every single newspaper in the UK and on television. It would be very difficult for them to back out now.

We reckoned we could buy the business for the headline price Travelodge needed, which was £50 million. We would put down £40 million and owe them £10 million. There was my £5 million and the Anglo-Irish bank's £39 million, totalling £44 million. We would pay Travelodge £40 million, and there would be £2 million in total fees, meaning we would have £2 million in the bank on day one.

Immediate running costs were not a problem. We had already ascertained that the cash flow from Little Chef was £2 million per week, so we would have plenty of working capital before we had to start paying out costs, once we took possession of the business.

A week of intense negotiation followed, at Travelodge's head office in London. In the final negotiations, we said, "Whatever you think, you can't get blood from a stone. That's all we've got."

So we settled on £51.5 million, which was an £8.5 million reduction from our initial bid. Those visits to restaurants all over the country had been worth it, because a good portion of the money saved would be needed to repair roofs and address all the other issues we found.

Then, three days before the deal was to be completed, I was at a charity event for the children's hospital in Sheffield when Anglo Irish Bank rang me on my cell phone. I took the phone call purely because I recognized their number. It was bad news. They said they had changed their minds; they wanted another £3 million personal guarantee from me.

This really pissed me off, because we'd already made a deal, and I never forgave them for that. Since I had spoken with them on a weekly basis, they knew that we had already spent £1.2 million on costs and were clearly committed to the deal. They used that opportunity to screw an extra £3 million guarantee out of me, which was unacceptable behavior. It was particularly annoying that they asked for a personal guarantee rather than cash. They knew I could give it to them because it wasn't going to cost me anything unless it went wrong; I didn't have to immediately come up with the cash.

So I had to put up £5 million in cash and a £3 million personal guarantee. I reluctantly agreed because I had no choice. I was absolutely sure I was going to turn Little Chef around. I was fully committed, hook, line, and sinker. We completed the deal in the early hours of one morning in London. We were off and running, the proud owners of an iconic British brand, with all the stress it was going to bring.

CHAPTER 6

LITTLE CHEF: THE SALE AND LEASEBACK

After the grueling ordeal, we were finally off and running with Little Chef. My hard work, taking a close look at the business, was now paying dividends. Visiting almost all of the units during the two months of the due diligence period gave me an opportunity to figure out what we were going to do with each outlet. Like any business, whether food, retail or technology, Little Chef followed the 80/20 rule – 80 percent of the profits came from 20 percent of the outlets.

At that time, Little Chef was turning over £100 million a year, so each week we had £2 million of cash coming through the door. So, it wasn't long before we went from having £2 million in the bank to £5 million. Of course, we had staff to pay and some rent to cover, but those were all of our expenses.

That meant we had room to implement some fairly bold ideas. Our first thought was that we wanted to offer something attractive and new to every unit, every manager, every member of staff, and – not least – every single customer. The only way we could do that was to make some radical changes, and that started with the menu. We decided to offer better-quality, healthier food. We put more salads on the menu, better quality bacon and sausages and healthier recipes and ingredients in general. We brought down the price of tea and coffee, since those were often what got people in the door in the first place, and we attracted more business with special offers, such as fish and chips for two for £5.

Next, we offered better value for money by bringing down not only the price of coffee and tea, but some of the ridiculous prices, such as a plate of chips for which Little Chef was charging £1.50, when you could get the same at any High Street corner chip shop for 50p. When marketing those special offers, we made a special effort to draw attention to the fact that we had changed our menu, hoping to bring back customers who hadn't been to Little Chef in years. Although we had been working on these plans prior to the purchase, it took about a month after the sale to instigate them.

But we needed to get the word out. How would we announce these innovations if we couldn't afford to go on national television or take out big newspaper advertisements? We decided to do it through the signage at the sites. Since millions of people drove past Little Chefs every week, it was an effective way to broadcast the message that Little Chef had changed. We called upon two guys who had been with us at Out of Town Restaurants who were very influential and knowledgeable. Kelvin McGowan looked deeply into how to improve the actual food we served, and he changed the menus to fit our new vision. Chris Andrew

Arthur researched and formulated the technology and pricing changes for the units.

Chris will always hold a special place in my heart. Not giving anything away, Chris was well overweight. On one occasion, I put together a staff team-building event in Derbyshire. It was a course where you had to climb along ropes and go through lakes and such. I had forgotten that one of the tasks was getting through a tunnel. There were a number of us there that day. Chris being the size he was, should never have gone near that tunnel because there was no way he was going to get through it successfully.

But, being a trooper, he did his best – and got stuck in the tunnel. We honestly wondered if we were going to have to call the fire brigade to dismantle the whole thing. I felt terrible for him. But once Chris became free, he came over and hugged me. He said that he would never forget it. That's the kind of guy I was excited to have back on my team for Little Chef.

Just 30 days after we closed the deal, we sounded the starting gun on the improved Little Chef – fully implemented new menus, special offers and better value, and signage all over the country. The signage cost about £10,000 per unit. Multiplied by 233 sites, it was a lot of money, a big investment. But it worked wonders. Customer numbers immediately went up substantially. We made these changes during the winter months, which were not the busiest, but at least we were seeing progress.

Even better, for the first time in years, the feedback left on the customer questionnaire sheets was positive.

Another addition we wanted to make was inspired by BP, which had successfully established a chain of on-the-go food and drink outlets called Wild Bean Café at filling stations. At the time, these takeaways weren't available at every single location as they are today.

I wanted to invest in similar takeaway facilities, so that people could buy a snack or a drink on the go. Times had changed dramatically since Little Chef got its start. People weren't in a rush back then. Now they're on their phones; they want to be moving. We believed that we could capture some of these customers who were in a hurry by implementing takeaway products at some of the Little Chefs where there was space. So we chose 30 sites to start with. Instead of partnering with an existing brand, we decided to create our own takeaway brand, called Coffee Tempo.

We met with the person who had put BP's whole Wild Bean operation together, Nick Smith, and asked him to join our team as development director, in charge of designing the initiative. The only problem was that we didn't have the cash to make it happen. He came aboard on a wing and a prayer – on the promise that we were going to get the money.

So David Coffer and I sat down to figure out how we were going to get the £5 million it would cost to open these 30 Coffee Tempos. I couldn't do it from cash flow, because we had already spent that money on the signage, menus, development, and people. David had a great idea – he suggested a sale and leaseback arrangement with the Little Chef properties we owned outright. That meant we would sell the 55 freeholds and lease them back. David believed it was a good plan since the property market was strong and everybody was familiar with Little Chef.

Many of the Travelodges situated next to Little Chefs had already done a sale and leaseback deal with Nick Leslau of the Prestbury Group, one of the biggest property companies in Britain. Therefore, he was an ideal buyer. David put together a sales brochure for all 55 units and we went out to the marketplace. Nick Leslau, the preferred buyer, quickly agreed to buy them for £55 million, which was the valuation that CBRE had initially made.

Nick Leslau became the sole buyer for the due diligence period. This was the first time that Simon and I had done a sale and leaseback of this nature, and he ended up tearing us apart. He found out that some of David Coffer's details were not accurate – from the size of some of the units to the size of the land to the number of car park spaces. He taught us the hard way about the importance of requesting environmental health studies for each unit. In the instances where we didn't have all the information that he wanted, we had to go out and get it.

Eventually, just before Christmas, he reduced his offer to £52 million. He assumed we would accept his deal and announced it to the press. *Property Week* and all the newspapers ran headlines about how Leslau bought the Little Chef freeholds for Christmas! So he was in for a real shock when we told him to go screw himself. We weren't taking his deal. He looked like a complete fool when we pulled out. Christmas came and we had no sale and leaseback and no Coffee Tempos. But we'd learned many lessons for the future.

I thank Nick for what he did, because he taught us what was wrong with our sales package. By January 10, we were able to amend these errors and go back out to the market. Straight away, commercial property businesses queued up to buy the freeholds. Arazim, an Israeli company, claimed that they could complete a deal in ten days. We believed what they were telling us, and more importantly, David Coffer believed them. I was eager to move ahead with our plans and, after Nick Leslau had spent two months messing us about, we were keen to finalise this one way or another. They were as good as their word, and the sale went through.

Not only did we now have cash to put into the Coffee Tempo rollout, the sale-and-leaseback arrangement meant we removed all debt from the company, leading to an increase in year-on-year cash flow.

Even better, the amount we were paying in rent on the sale and leaseback was 20 percent less than the amount we were paying in interest and capital on the company's debt when we owned the properties. It was the perfect deal for Little Chef in every possible way.

When the money came in, we already had everything in place – all the plans, the builders, and the designs. So we started to open Coffee Tempo at all the chosen sites. We selected busy, successful outlets with adequate space. Many were high-profile sites on dual carriageways, scattered across the country.

We didn't open them all on one day, but over the period of the next few months, and sales were good. People who had traditionally come in just to use the toilets started buying a coffee or a sandwich. However, this did affect sales at the sit-down Little Chefs. The overall picture was better, but some people were grabbing and going, rather than eating at the restaurant, despite our new and improved menu.

So we spent the £5 million, had cash coming in, and then we knew that the big moment was coming – summertime. That was when 80 percent of all profits were earned at Little Chef, because that's when people went on holiday. There was still an impression by people who had not visited in a while, or who had never visited, that the food was not that good and the pricing poor. We needed a better public profile.

Throughout May and June, I wrestled with what should be our next big idea to attract the British public into Little Chefs. We didn't have any money for advertising, and I needed to come up with an initiative that was free. I wanted to bring this beloved brand back to the minds of the British people, many of whom who really wanted us to succeed. That was the key thing. Everybody I spoke to – customers, staff, members of the public – all said, "We just want Little Chef to be back where it was, and we want to go there and enjoy it instead of it being run down. We want to go back and love it. Just do something with it!"

So I decided to go for the jugular. I had an idea that was going to create chaos. There would be a national outcry. But as they say, there's no such thing as bad publicity. It would put Little Chef on everybody's mind. People would stop in just because they read about it every day in the newspapers. And that's exactly what we needed.

I was going to go on national television – all the national television channels were lined up, as well as all the newspaper editors – and explain that I had interviewed thousands and thousands of people who all wanted Little Chef to work. But at the moment, 250,000 people were stopping there each week, and only 125,000 of them were spending any money. The rest were "spending a penny." That wasn't enough to sustain Little Chef's toilets, let alone the business as a whole.

One of the biggest customer complaints was that the toilets were run-down. That's because the people using the toilets weren't even customers! They were just people using the toilets. I decided to announce that, because so many people use the toilets without buying anything, we didn't have the money to invest back in the toilets.

From the start of the school holidays and on, we would have a new rule. People must either pay 50p to use the toilet or spend a minimum of 50p at Little Chef. It was another opportunity to highlight the new menus, the new food, and the Coffee Tempos. We would show them that we were turning the place around, but we needed their support to continue. This is what people said they wanted. Now was their chance to come back. They could visit while traveling around the country during the holiday period. They could put Little Chef back on the map.

There really wasn't anywhere else to go to the toilet on the A roads in those days. People who needed the toilet and wanted to stay on their route would have to come in and buy a cup of tea or coffee, or a Bradwell's Ice Cream, just for the chance to use the toilet. I firmly believed, after running all the numbers, that we would be able to add £3 million profit to the bottom line just from the new toilet charge, which would have helped with the rollout of the Coffee Tempos.

The second controversial thing that I wanted to do was to change the Fat Charlie logo. Throughout the history of Little Chef, this fat chef has been on every sign and every menu. He was a very well-known and well-loved mascot. The day I purchased Little Chef, we got a lot of press. The headline on the *Financial Times* said, "Wosskow buys Little Chef," with a picture of the Little Chef sign. The first text I got on my phone was from a friend having a laugh: "How the hell did they get you up there on that sign so quickly?" It was funny because even though I've always been quite fit, I also have a little belly.

For years, people had commented on his image. As I said earlier, an attempt to slim him down, just a year or so before we bought Little Chef, was abandoned after negative reactions from customers. But I was determined to actually change it. I believed we should create a fitter, healthier, more fun image to represent Little Chef, and I was really excited about it. I knew that, once the whole outcry had calmed down about charging people to use the toilets, people would be excited about this new move. Little Chef was going to stay in the news, one way or another! I was going to wait until our busiest time, at the end of July – two weeks after the toilet announcement – to announce that we were changing Fat Charlie.

In order to generate buzz and enthusiasm for the idea of updating Fat Charlie, we were going to hold a competition with a £100,000 first prize for the person who could come up with the best logo and branding for the company. Our company was now called the People's Restaurant Group, and the message was that we were inclusive, inviting the people of Great Britain to have a say in the company's motto. This would, of course, also get us a ton of free publicity.

The announcements were planned for July 10, just five days prior to the start of the school holidays. My days started at five in the morning in the months leading up to the planned media coup. Either I went to the head office or visited the sites. I needed to find out how people were reacting to the new menus, and the only way to get an honest sense of how effective they were was to talk to customers and staff. I also wanted to see the signage in each place, to decide how we could change it to best promote the new menus and special offers. We were still identifying more sites suitable for the new fast food facilities and Coffee Tempos. There was so much to do. Seven days a week, I worked from 5:00 a.m. to midnight. And then, just nine days before the plan to take the British media by storm was enacted, everything came to a screeching halt.

CHAPTER 7

LITTLE CHEF: THE HEART ATTACK

Many people have asked me what it feels like to have a heart attack. And I've read a slew of personal accounts that suggest that everyone has a slightly different experience. Most of the people who have asked me are around the age of 50 and male, who are obviously worried about themselves and symptoms they've experienced.

One thing it's certainly not is a sharp pain that lasts a few seconds in your chest. That could mean you've pulled a muscle or tendon, or a variety of other things. That's not a heart attack. In my case, the heart attack started with indigestion, leading to pains in my left arm, which then led to pains in my chest, which also led to nausea and sweating.

Anybody experiencing those symptoms for more than a few minutes should not do what I did and arrive at the hospital by car, hours later. Call the emergency services immediately and save your life, or the life of somebody else experiencing those symptoms. What's clear is that the sooner you can get to a hospital with the correct staffing and facilities to treat you, the more likely it is that they can save your life and mitigate the amount of damage done to your heart if you survive.

The heart attack that stopped me in my tracks on July 1, 2006, was the most critical event of my life, and probably the biggest cock-up in the way that it was handled. I made some colossal mistakes, as did the people who were treating me in the hospital in every capacity. Do not do what I did. I had way too many hours to sit and wonder if I was going to make it through the night. I wouldn't wish that upon anyone.

Obviously, the more hours that passed, the more chance I had to survive. They made it clear that the most critical times were during the heart attack and immediately afterwards. We all know that 50 percent of people die instantly or within 24 hours of a heart attack. So the odds that they gave me of a 50/50 survival rate were a fair assumption. And, it was especially bad luck for me coming in on a Saturday night, because there was no cardiologist on call, at all. Thankfully, I had a doctor friend in Sheffield who specialized in cardiology. I called him and he directed the young doctor who was tending me on Sunday as to what drugs to administer.

Finally, a cardiologist came to see me on Monday. He explained that I had an almost complete blockage in the left side of my heart and would be transferred to Harefield Heart Hospital nearby.

I arrived at the specialized hospital on July 5, 2006, which just happened to be my 43rd birthday. As in Hillingdon, there was no working air conditioning to counter the stifling heat inside – a shambles! They took me into the operating theatre and told Julie that the procedure would take a maximum of 90 minutes.

The surgeon kept me awake while attempting to insert a stent (a piece of metal that keeps the arteries open) into my heart. The surgeon asked his assistant for a certain size. A few minutes later the assistant came back and explained that they were out of stock of that size. The doctor asked for a different size, but that was also out of stock.

Growing frustrated, he asked for the nearest size. Unfortunately, after inserting it, he found that it did not cover the whole area where the artery was ruptured. So he asked for a bigger stent, which he tried next. He looked unhappy and called another expert for a second opinion. We had already been there for two hours.

Little did I know that Julie was experiencing more trauma than I was. When she asked about my condition, the nurse got me mixed up with another grey-haired patient. That man had serious complications and was having an emergency bypass. So Julie panicked unnecessarily while the doctors played musical stents with my heart.

Back in the operating theatre, the doctor explained that since he had not had the correct size stents, he had inadvertently torn the artery when inserting the second stent. He was now going to insert a third stent, a much larger one. It worked. Despite the odds, I had made it through the critical period. But I can't say my opinion of the National Health Service was improved. With all illnesses, determination to persevere and physical fitness play a role in your chances of recovery. I have no doubt whatsoever – and I thought about this a lot that first night – that all of the work that tested my endurance and the rigorous physical activity I'd done throughout my lifetime were bound to help my chances of surviving this particular situation. During the many hours when I was unsure if I'd make it through the night, I had a lot of time to reflect on those nearest and dearest to me. Of course, I spent a great deal of time imagining what would happen to Julie and the kids. Julie is my left arm, and I am Julie's right arm. We've spent so much time together since the age of 17 that it would be very, very difficult for one of us to lose the other.

But at the same time, I had no doubt that Julie would survive and battle through the massive loss for our children, Hannah and Toby. And since she is such a great mother and inspiration to them, they would all survive the bereavement.

On my telephone conversation with Julie that horrible night, I told her that she must tell the children that if this was the last time she spoke to me, my only wish for the future was that they would grow up to be best friends and look after each other until they left this earth. And those words were repeated to them by Julie *verbatim*. I am happy to say that my ultimate dream among all dreams has been realized. Today, Hannah and Toby are the best of friends. Their mutual respect for one another is unrivaled; Hannah runs every important decision she makes by Toby, and vice versa.

At the hospital that night, I had the chance to make two phone calls. The first was to Julie, and the second was to my best friend, Tim Ralston from Sheffield. I asked Tim to make the speech at my funeral, if that's how the events played out.

"Of course, I'll do it," he said.

"What are you going to say?" I asked.

"I'll tell the mourners that they should not feel sorry for Lawrence. He already lived the equivalent of 500 years for a normal human being in his 43 years." That made me laugh, when I needed it most.

The next weekend my other best friend, Nidge, was getting married, and I was supposed to be best man. Whether I made it through the night or not, I knew I wouldn't be able to perform my duties. So I asked Tim to step in for me. He duly accepted, and took the initiative to dress the part, impersonating me. He made the whole speech with a grey mop on his head and a large false nose. I cracked up when he came to visit and showed me the video.

Luckily, Tim never had to make his other speech. The next few months were challenging, to say the least, with frequent visits to the hospital and constant worries. When I left Harefield, I was told that a third of my heart had been lost. But six weeks after the heart attack, I took a treadmill to 15 minutes, the maximum, which absolutely amazed the doctor. He explained that there was no way I had lost a third of my heart, which was very uplifting news for me. The bad news was that he told me that I absolutely could not go back to work for a minimum of 12 months. With no family history of heart failure, no smoking, no drugs, and excellent fitness, the reason I had nearly lost my life was stress. There was no doubt about that. There's a good reason why they call stress the silent killer.

Anxiety continued to be a problem. Perhaps understandably, I had panic attacks whenever I felt any pain, imagining another heart attack was happening to me. This was not good, because it raised my heartbeat beyond the rate doctors wanted to see. Severe anxiety symptoms lasted with me for months and sometimes became debilitating. During my months of recovery time, when I had virtually none of my previous responsibilities to attend to, I sat outside watching the clouds. It's true that I took a break for a while after the sale of Out of Town Restaurants Group, but this was the first time in my life that I was forced, under doctor's orders, to do nothing. My dream was unravelling. I couldn't help restlessly thinking about what I would be doing to help Little Chef if I was working. I had little bits of information from conversations with Simon, but I wasn't supposed to be involved on a day-to-day basis, or to follow what was going on too closely.

In my absence, my revolutionary ideas for getting tons of attention for Little Chef, by introducing a charge to use the toilets and reinventing Fat Charlie, did not come to fruition. Those changes would have been massive, and the owner – the person driving the whole operation – wasn't there to inspire any confidence. The situation was too tentative and chaotic for it to be a good time to make big changes with confidence. Instead, the focus was far too much on my absence. Everybody was asking, "Is Lawrence dead? Is he alive? What's going to happen?"

We based our projected profits on 2006, which had been a good summer. Unfortunately, the summer of 2007 brought lashings of rain. People didn't travel, so they didn't go to Little Chef as much. The numbers, during that critical summer period where we should have made most of our profit, were poor.

Simon at that point held 10 percent of The People's Restaurant Group, which I had given him in the same spirit that I gave Richard 10 percent of Out of Town. He was an amazing guy, a financial wizard, but he didn't have the same entrepreneurial spirit I had. We were great when we worked together; if we could have continued an active partnership, things would have been great. But neither of us was capable of turning the business around on our own. Things would have turned out exactly the same if I had been left to run Little Chef alone; it wouldn't have worked. Little Chef needed both of us, and we needed each other.

I've seen before what happens when entrepreneurs leave their businesses. Once that leader – that driver, that inspiration – isn't there, things are not the same. Even if you've got a great team – which we were still building – the heartbeat stops pumping a sense of purpose and inspiration through the system. Simon did his absolute best, but Little Chef's figures remained down on the year. I was crestfallen. I was also severely frustrated that I couldn't come back and make things right.

So I was in the perfect state of mind to welcome an apparent white knight into the fray. Just at that time, an old friend from junior school, James Burdall, came back into my life. I had reconnected with him a year earlier on a coast-to-coast UK bike ride, and he came to see me often during my recovery. He had a lot of time on his hands, since the businesses he owned weren't very time-consuming. My best friends Nigel, Tim, and Nick were busy working their butts off, so I appreciated the company of someone who knew me from way back when I was just a kid with dreams of making it big.

He was very kind to me after the heart attack. He kindly and attentively accompanied me on my first walk outside, as well as my first bike ride. He spent hours working with me on my physical rehab. For six months, he spent hours every day helping me, both physically and mentally. We became very close and built up significant trust very quickly. Little did I know that his kindness was a ruthlessly calculated sham, just his way of getting inside my affairs when I was at my most vulnerable.

After the first six months of recovery, blissfully unaware of the cuckoo I had let into my nest, I got the all-clear to travel. As soon as I could, we took the kids out of school and headed for our holiday home in Orlando, Florida. It was a welcome escape from all the trauma back home, and an opportunity to utilize the American healthcare system.

I kept in touch with Simon throughout the autumn and into winter, and he told me things were not good. He had lined up an administrator to get rid of loss-making units. In the restaurant business, cash flow is everything. Once it rises above the point where your overheads are covered, profit margins are very high. By the same token, if you don't take in as much cash, your profit quickly disappears. The decline in business during that period meant a drop in cash flow, and that in turn halted the expansion of Coffee Tempos. I increasingly got the impression that the people who were left behind without me were slipping into survival mode. September, October, and November brought improved results, but the damage from the disappointing summer trade had been done.

Without my entrepreneurial spirit to guide the company towards more creative, bold solutions, the people left behind had to fall back on their wisdom and experience on the financial side. They decided to engineer a financial scenario that would land them a bigger shareholder. By December, the focus became selling the business, and therefore figuring out what they could do to replace me, in order to make the business more attractive.

Simon rang me between Christmas and the New Year to tell me he had lined up a buyer – RCapital, a private investment group that specialized in business turnaround. I could hardly blame him and the rest of the team for bailing out. The storm of Little Chef's financial struggles had hit the headlines in every newspaper in the UK. On December 30, 2006, the only news on BBC Worldwide ahead of the Little Chef story was Saddam Hussein being put to death! The deal Simon had negotiated would save most of the five thousand jobs across Little Chef; nothing would really change for the employees. That was my main concern, so I was relieved.

But I was also angry. I know that I could have sorted the business out. It would have been difficult; it would have been a lot of hard work, but it was sortable. There was so much to work with. Little Chef had 93 percent name recognition. It was like Coca-Cola – a brand that everybody loved, everybody knew growing up, and everybody wanted to believe in. That was my driving motivation. I named our company The People's Restaurant Group because I truly believed Little Chef belonged to The People.

Little Chef was not disposable; it was an icon. It was the British people's restaurant, where we'd all gone while on holiday. I truly felt the will of the people was in favor of it. All I had to do was get those hundreds of thousands of people who had given up on it because it was so bad for so long to come back and try it and have a decent experience. I was convinced I could convert them into return customers because, in their heart of hearts, they longed to like it and for it to be as good as they remembered. There are few brands that carry anything like that amount of good will and positive association. There was just a sheer will for Little Chef to be successful that was unlike anything I'd ever seen. There was even a nationalistic element. If a customer could choose

American Starbucks or British Little Chef, they'd choose Little Chef all day long. All that was required was that it be up to standard. But that didn't happen, and so began its long and painful decline. I may not have had the opportunity to save Little Chef, but I did have the rare opportunity to live a second life. In theory, it was a heavenly prospect – leaving behind the stress of running too fast, too long, to run too many businesses. I prepared myself for the unknown.

CHAPTER 8

THE FULL MONTY:

101 THINGS TO DO BEFORE I DIE

I saw that it was time to move on to the next phase of my life, and achieve new and different goals. It was now clear to me that I had a non-negotiable, inborn tendency to seek out activities that really made the adrenaline pump, in order to damp down an intense, underlying, hereditary anxiety. The stress that came with doing thrillingly impossible business deals allowed me to manage my anxiety, but it came close to straining my body to a near-fatal breaking point. It was time to count my blessings and pursue excitement in other forms.

I bought a book called *In the Playground of the Gods*, about a sports journalist who was not good enough at any one sport to become a professional, but wanted to play with the best and live the life of a full-time, competitive sportsman. Along with the book I had purchased in New York, *101 Things To Do Before You Die*, it helped me draw up my own list. I called it "The Full Monty: 101 Things To Do Before I Die".

In achieving these goals, I wanted to help others less fortunate than me, wherever possible, while creating the adrenaline I craved. I wanted to use my learnings to help others and give back, but also to create at least some excitement for myself. I was dead set on enjoying new and ambitious experiences centered around two of my passions: sport and music.

I had to be careful, however, to schedule these goals around my recovering health. Although my heart was improving as each month passed by, a sudden pain or a rapid heart-beat could put me on the edge of panic. For the whole of that first year after my heart attack, there was not one minute that passed that I did not think about my heart in some way.

A lot of people ask me what it's like to have a heart attack, and I tell them, of course, about the warning signs I ignored, the importance of recognizing them, and of getting medical attention as soon as possible.

But in many ways, the worst part was the aftermath. The fear of it happening again caused me to panic, regularly. And the panic would make me think maybe I was having another heart attack! Meanwhile, I was on forced rest. I was forbidden to work for a year and then told not to get actively involved in business for three years. I couldn't really do much of anything. I was scared, and my energy levels were very low at times – a symptom of the drugs I was now taking and knew I would have to take for the rest of my life. I couldn't do much to get fitter and more active, because the doctors were very strict with me about keeping my activities to a minimum.

For a whole year, it was all about getting well, and the constant fear of having another heart attack made it one of the worst years of my life. Worse, I couldn't resist following the dismal tale of what was going on at Little Chef, absent my guiding vision. RCapital, the UK private equity group, paid less than £10 million for it in January 2007, which really broke my heart. The 38 branches that were not included in the sale were closed immediately; the remaining 217 restaurants continued to operate normally. Things went downhill from there. By December 2007 a number of Little Chefs not leased from Travelodge or Arazim (the two main landlords) closed, as Little Chef had not been able to reach agreements with those individual landlords. Then, during 2008 and 2009, all the franchised outlets at Moto sites closed.

After the sale, the new owners attracted celebrity chef Heston Blumenthal for the Channel 4 series "Big Chef takes on Little Chef." The show chronicled his attempts to revamp the A303 branch at Popham, Hampshire. Blumenthal's new menu included delicacies like ox cheeks and spit-roast chicken. Strawberry and orange flower water yoghurts were on the breakfast menu, a far cry from the beloved Jubilee Pancakes.

The owners promised that if Blumenthal's redesign and new offerings were profitable, the format would be incorporated at all the branches. He also made changes to the décor, and personal touches to everything including urinals that played recordings of Spike Milligan reciting nonsense verse. His model never spread to all the sites, but they were implemented in eleven of them.

Swanky branding agency Venture Three was hired to conduct a wide scale rebranding effort that included a digital campaign on Twitter and Facebook. None of their efforts seemed to make much of a difference. They were trying to bang a square peg into a round hole. People wanted to reconnect with their memories of long road trips with their grandparents, not trendy dishes from a three-Michelin-starred chef. In January of 2012, Little Chef announced that they planned to close 67 of the chain's failing restaurants. By June of 2013, they eliminated all of Heston Blumenthal's creations from the menus.

Little Chef fell further down in its fortunes. In July 2013, the current administration brought in another takeover by Kout Food Group from Kuwait. The chain went from 439 restaurants at the peak to just 78 today. I still truly believe that if it wasn't for my heart attack, I was one of the very few people who could have turned this iconic brand around. Unfortunately, fate intervened.

The chain appeared in terminal decline. I felt thoroughly depressed by the world in general.

All this just pushed me harder to get off my backside and go and do some good for others less fortunate than me, while at the same time helping myself. After I'd done my year of sitting around like a miserable lump, I managed to prove to my doctors that I'd substantially recovered. My heart function was far better than they had hoped, and I was actually in pretty good shape. But I couldn't work. That's why I turned to focusing on the 101 things to do before I died (hoping that was now some good way off), while raising money for charity. With the doctors' approvals I started on my quest. I couldn't start my own charity – that was beyond me. But I could make a contribution to other people's organizations. So I mixed fund-raising activities with challenges that would complete my list.

It took a while to figure out how to get started, but on a trip to Las Vegas, I became friends with a casino manager at the Bellagio Resort. Lucky for me, his wife was personal assistant to Andre Agassi, who happens to be my favorite tennis player. I have always loved his "never say die" attitude.

When I shared my vision of living like an athlete while doing good, my friend suggested I visit the K-12 charity-based school Andre had set up locally. It is called The Andre Agassi College Preparatory Academy, and it gives the poorest kids in Las Vegas a second chance in life, an opportunity to excel and attend college. These kids came from broken homes. Some were beaten and sexually abused; they suffered all kinds of setbacks. As soon as I visited the school, I fell in love with the work Andre and his team were doing. Here was a charity project I could really get my teeth into.

I managed to wangle an invitation to Andre's charity event that night and, deploying even more of the Wosskow charm, I was able to meet Andre and Steffi in the flesh. It was an especially spectacular evening to encounter them. That night they raised $18 million, which made it one of the most successful charity events in history at the time. They raised $9 million during the evening, and then the founder of Beanie Babies, Ty Warner, got up on stage and doubled it, which was incredible.

One of the items that raised money at the event was the auctioning off of a week with Andre and Steffi on holiday at Sea Island, off the coast of Georgia, US, as well as an opportunity to play tennis with them. Julie and I bid hard, and we won. It was the beginning of a genuine friendship; during that week on Sea Island, my relationship with Andre was cemented. I've always loved tennis and I've always loved Andre, so playing him was a dream come true. I'm a 4.0 (out of 7) on the National Tennis Rating Program scale, which is considered "good", although below college tournament standard. Andre, of course, is a 7 – a world class champion who was ranked No. 3 in the world by the age of 18. He agreed to play me with his off-hand – his left instead of his right - and still beat me 6-0. It just shows you how good he is. Being on the receiving end of one of those famous two-handed backhanders, hit right down the line, will take your breath away.

As my relationship with Andre grew stronger throughout the years, I continued supporting the school. Attending graduation for the first class of students, in 2009, was a deeply moving experience. These kids had been headed for the trash heap; now they were going off to schools like Stanford, Harvard, and Yale. What a difference Andre – a high school dropout himself – made!

Julie and me with the Agassi's

I was getting the feel for fund-raising now and turned my attention to the next sport – football. My ambition was to hold a charity match where we could raise money, and I would actually get to play. When Doncaster Rovers were closing their old ground down to move to a new one, I saw a perfect opportunity to make this happen.

I approached the chairman, who was a friend of mine, and said, "I'd like to put together a Sheffield United all-star team made up of half professionals and half amateurs, and all proceeds would go to charity." He thought it was a great idea.

We arranged the event and, to my astonished delight, five thousand people attended. We raised £50,000 that night. My dream came true when I scored the goal that took the game to penalties. So that was the football conquest ticked from my list. That wasn't the end of football-related fun, though. I'm a real die-hard fan.

In 2003, my beloved team, Sheffield United, had made it through to the playoffs that would potentially take them to the Premier League.

One night, they had an event to raise money for charity, and the team's manager, Neil Warnock, was auctioning off a bottle of champagne he'd been given for being Manager of the Month. The bid, driven by me, went up to £800, but Neil was unhappy about that because the manager of rival team, Sheffield Wednesday, had raised £1,200 from his bottle. I told Neil I would buy the bottle for £1,500 if he would agree to let Toby and me come to the final game before the playoffs, which was being played at Watford, traveling with them on the team coach. I've learned a lot in this phase of my life about people, and how warm-hearted they can be when it comes to raising money for charity. Neil's good nature (and refusal to be outdone by Sheffield Wednesday's manager) kicked in and he said yes.

It was one of the best things I have ever done. The players absolutely loved having Toby and me there, especially Toby, who was all of ten, and started a food fight at dinner the night before the match. The next day, before the match, just for fun, Toby was allowed to take penalty kicks against Sheffield United's goalie. By now, he was such a Team Mascot that every time the goalie saved one, the crowd would boo, but every time he let one of Toby's kicks in, there were huge cheers. I don't think I've ever seen Toby happier.

As a side note, another similar incident showed me how different people can be. At a similar charity event years later, I bought the same sort of fun package to travel with Manchester United when they flew to Athens for a match against Olympiakos in the Champions League. What a difference. Those overpaid, supposed superstars were barely able to bring themselves to talk to me. What a disappointment. I can't say I'm sorry they got thrashed 2-nil, with an extra goal against them in injury time. With many sport-related goals already in the bag, it was time to turn my attention to music. If there was no limit to my dreams coming true, how about I might meet my absolute favorite musician of all – Elton John? I truly love his music, and I have so much respect for the fact that he's given his life over to his AIDS Foundation, about which he is so deeply passionate.

In the early 90s, while governments and the healthcare industry were still down-playing the urgency of recognizing, treating and preventing AIDS, Elton saw an opportunity to use his money and influence to bring the issue into the spotlight. He established a foundation in the US in 1992 and the UK in 1993, attracting such luminary patrons as Sting, Boris Becker, Annie Lennox, David and Victoria Beckham, and Emma Thompson. The Elton John AIDS Foundation Academy Award Party, started in 1993, is held every year in LA, following the Oscars ceremony, and is one of the most high-profile parties in the Hollywood film industry. Both foundations continue to fight for the dignity and well-being of every person, combat stigma, prevent HIV infections, ensure universal HIV treatment for all who need it, and pressure governments to end AIDS. Altogether, after nearly 25 years of fund-raising and activism, the foundations have raised $350 million. The US foundation, which focuses its efforts on programs in the United States, the Americas, and the Caribbean, was recently recognized by Funders for LGBTQ Issues as the largest funder of LGBTQ health programs in the nation and by Funders Concerned About AIDS as the largest HIV funder of programs for transgender people. Elton is not just someone I admired because of his musical talents and showmanship; he also does more good in the world than most people I have met put together.

Again, fortune smiled on my boldness and, through Andre Agassi, I met Billie Jean King, who gave me the chance to meet my idol at his house in Windsor. From that day onwards, I managed to get to know him and become his friend.

Sir Elton John, Billie Jean King, and Andre Agassi, the three leaders of the charities we have helped the most

I hope you know enough about me by now to gather that I'm a man who loves to form relationships, but I want to emphasize that cultivating this particular friendship has been one of the great joys of my life. I felt we hit it off right away and, after making that initial contact, I wanted to cement the friendship. Billie Jean King's charity, Smash Hits, was auctioning off a chance to have lunch with Elton at one of their events, and Julie and I bought it. We cashed in our lunch date during one of our trips to Las Vegas with Hannah and Toby. However, he surprised us by inviting us to his hotel suite. We presumed that we would just go for lunch, and then leave. We were wrong! The lunch started at 12:30 p.m., and we stayed all day until right before his show at 7:30 p.m.

The conversation was amazing. We discussed his relationship with John Lennon, with Princess Diana, and with Gianni Versace. All three were tragically killed, which had a profound impact on his life. He talked about how he felt at Diana's funeral and how he held himself together, before eventually breaking down on the long drive home. So many topics were covered that afternoon – marriage, children, being gay, the AIDS Foundation, being knighted by the Queen. He told us about the boy from New Zealand who changed his life. He opened up about his temperaments and his moods, what made him moody, and how his children had now settled him down. It was pure magic.

At the end of the afternoon, I said to Elton, "I've got to get us back to our hotel, changed, showered, and ready to come watch your show. Even though you could probably sit here all day and arrive ten minutes before it starts, we can't."

He really didn't want us to go. It was so nice for him to be with four other down-to-earth Brits with whom he was comfortable and felt free to say whatever he wanted. From spending time with celebrities, I know that, for somebody in his position, this is rare. People get very nervous around famous people. They try to be something they're not in order to make a great impression, and their nerves tend to drive them to do and say ridiculous things they would never otherwise do or say. That's really uncomfortable to be around. Or else they're calculating and figuring out how they can get something from the celebrity, like an endorsement, or money, or sex. But the Wosskow family doesn't act different with anyone. I've truly raised my kids to be proud of who they are naturally, and Julie and I have never put on airs and graces. Elton really responded to that. And although no confidences will be broken, he told us some very interesting stories – including a hilarious one about a face-off with the Queen. I mean, the actual Queen!

At the show that night, Elton introduced one of his songs by saying it was a tribute to four of the nicest people he'd ever met in his life: the Wosskow family. Then he sang "Don't Let the Sun Go Down On Me." It meant so much to us. He then demanded that we go backstage and see him after the show, before we all left. What an incredible day that was.

A talented performer and wonderful person

This is another example of a relationship that ended up coming around full circle. Toby has become good friends with Jon Howard, one of Elton John's closest team members, and, through that relationship, he was given the opportunity to make one of Elton's music videos. The piece was about a father-son relationship and was released on Father's Day to my joy. Then, Jon introduced Toby to Scott Thompson, aka Carrot Top, who is the subject of Toby's documentary, which is currently in production

Undoubtedly, Toby is learning how to evolve relationships quickly too.

Elton John was also performing at an event I attended in St. Petersburg, Russia. Richard Caring, who had set up most of the manufacturing companies in the Far East to supply the now-disgraced Sir Philip Green with clothing for his BHS stores, decided to fly 450 of us out to St. Petersburg for three days, with the goal of raising more money in one evening than had ever been raised before, anywhere in the world, for the NSPCC.

The main party was held in the Yusopov Palace, which is a stunningly beautiful, Rococo and Moorish-style, 18th century jewel-box of a private palace steeped in history (it's where Rasputin was murdered). It has its own theatre in one of the wings. When we arrived, the Kirov Ballet was giving a private performance of "Swan Lake". I met President Bill Clinton and was able to talk to him about various charity movements in the world. Later, Elton John performed, too, and he was amazing, as ever.

All dressed up with Bill Clinton

But the highlight of the evening was near the end when Tina Turner, who had come out of retirement to perform the finale, sang "You're Simply the Best" to President Clinton. I was standing right next to him, so I could see the tears pour down his face. That evening, £30 million was raised to help combat abuse against children. And it was one of the most awe-inspiring parties I ever went to.

Charitable work led me to meet another of my great heroes – Muhammad Ali. I managed to get involved with organizing an event held in Scottsdale, Arizona, called "Escape for Good", set up to celebrate his 70th birthday.

My son Toby and I with the greatest, Muhammad Ali

The moment I found out I could get involved with this milestone event, I jumped at the chance. On top of the thrill of meeting my hero and raising some money, it was also a great opportunity to gather together a lot of influential people and put them somewhere for three days to brainstorm the future of charitable work. Of course, while they were there, we wanted to give them a fantastic time.

For me, the highlight of the weekend was with my son, Toby. He had just won, at 18, Best High School Drama award at the 2010 International Student Film Festival Hollywood, for his five-minute cautionary tale about not being able to outrun the past, "Coming to Terms" – a huge boost to his nascent film career. Recognizing the wind in Toby's sails, the main organizer of the event asked him to make a speech at Muhammad's 70th birthday party. It was, of course, a huge honour, but also a very daunting prospect, because he'd be delivering his speech in the company of some very famous people. We rehearsed together over and over in the days leading up to the party.

When Toby's big day came and we arrived at the party, we realized he was the youngest person in attendance, which raised the stakes even higher. A few minutes before Toby was due to speak, Tom Jackson, an NFL legend, happened to pass by. He couldn't help noticing a young man huddled over a piece of paper, looking very nervous, and he took the time to stop and find out what was going on. When Toby told him about the speech, Tom assured him that, if he let go of his inhibitions and spoke from the heart, his words would come naturally.

Toby took the advice thoroughly on board. He stood up and knocked 'em for six!

Toby's adventure wasn't over yet, though. A little later, it was Tom Jackson's turn to make his speech. He began by talking about a young man, Toby, and asked him to stand so everyone could see who he was talking about. He then related the story about reassuring Toby, and admitted that he, also, was nervous. This, from the former linebacker who was largely responsible for the Denver Broncos' unstoppable "Orange Crush Defense" that won them the 1987 Super Bowl, a modern-day Hercules! To hear him admit to being nervous about speaking in public was a revelation, not just to Toby, but pretty much everybody else.

As Toby sat back down, he looked to the next table to find Muhammad smiling at him. Muhammad lifted his hand, giving a little wave of approval, and Toby waved back. They shared a truly special moment.

It was the most inspiring event of Toby's young life. He became infatuated by Ali. He read every book about him, watched every documentary, and, eventually made his own short film about a young boy who was inspired by him. It was Toby's own letter of gratitude to The Champ.

On top of this, Escape for Good gave us the chance to cycle with Lance Armstrong, before his exploits became apparent. Racing with him was something of a lifelong dream for me.

Cycling with Lance Armstrong

Next, I organized the Ryder Cup equivalent at Isleworth, the community in Florida to which Julie and I had moved by then. The idea was to have 12 non-Americans play 12 Americans, and it went down really well. By now, I had joined Bay Hill, around the corner from Isleworth, which was a club owned by Arnold Palmer, who is generally regarded as one of the greatest players in the sport's history. I've always been fascinated by excellence, and it seemed amazing to be so close to a man who really was the living embodiment of that quality. I requested and was granted a meeting with Mr. Palmer, and we became friends. Now, I asked if I could organize our golf tournament there as well. He agreed.

The night before, he came to me and said, "Look, the bottom line is that you're the non-American captain, and I'm the American captain, so we're playing each other tomorrow." Memories of being thrashed by Andre Agassi came to mind. I reflected I should be more careful about what I wished for, such as a game of golf against the most formidable player that ever lived.

"I really don't want to play you," I said.

"Well, you're going to," he assured me, with a slap on the arm.

It turned out to be not at all what I was expecting. Mr. Palmer is such a gentleman, and a wonderful person. By the time we got to the 14th hole, I was beating him easily. He made a classic statement: "I hit the ball that far these days; I can hear it land!" We were both in a bunker at this point, about 150 feet away from the hole. When I chipped the ball straight in, he went to the golf cart and got the white towel and started waving it.

"Well done," he said. It was incredible. That was certainly one of my life's great moments. I was very sad to hear that this wonderful gentleman had passed away in September 2016.

The game of a lifetime with Arnold Palmer, a dear friend

Back to musical goals – this time to play in a band. Music is an enduring passion of mine, with the power to move me like it did that weekend when Freddie Mercury singing "I want to break free" emboldened me to make a brave and radical step in my life journey. Playing in a band was something I could get truly excited about. There was only one problem: I have absolutely no musical talent. I'm not being modest. When I was younger, I desperately tried to play one instrument after another – guitar, bass, drums, anything – and failed miserably. I can't sing, either. You'd rather listen to a cat caught in a tumble drier than hear my voice, I can assure you. So, years earlier, I'd accepted that I was never going to be part of a band.

But this was my new life, in which I could make dreams come true. And fate, it seems, was on my side. When Julie and I came to sell our house in Sheffield, the buyer turned out to be one of the band members of Sheffield's own Def Leppard. At the end of negotiations, we were down to a gap of £15,000, and I said, "I'll give you £7,500 off the price of the house, and I'll give the other £7,500 to a charity of your choice, if you'll let me come on tour with you."

That was how I came to find myself, dazed by stadium lights on an outdoor stage in Tampa, Florida, in front of 10,000 sweaty, heaving metal heads, miming like crazy with a guitar while Def Leppard did their thing around me. It really was an amazing experience, worth every penny. It was also a thoroughly good reminder that you should never say "never".

And then we were off to the races. Literally. As a youngster, I always enjoyed having a gamble on the horses and going to watch them. My favourite memories were from the August meeting at York Racecourse. My dream was to own a racehorse and win a race at York.

Julie, Hannah, Toby and I went out as a family and bought four racehorses, thereby getting the privilege of naming one each. Mine was Emerald Bay, named after a private community in Laguna Beach,

California, where we had bought a vacation house in years gone by. Julie's horse was Haunting Memories, Hannah's was Hannah's Dream, and Toby's was Toby's Dream. All four horses performed well, with three of them winning a race each, and the fourth coming in second in one race. The chances of winning a race when you buy a racehorse are 30 to 1, so we were delighted at the results.

A dream come true, the big winner at my favourite racecourse

One of my heroes in business and in horse-racing was Sheikh Mohammed Maktoum from Dubai. He helped turn a desert into one of the most exciting cities on earth, as well as launching a number of incredibly influential companies that really put Dubai on the business map – Emirates Airline, DP World and the Jumeirah Group. I visited Dubai many times over the course of 15 years and had been amazed to see it change so much. Sheikh Mohammed was not only a spectacular real-estate developer and entrepreneur (he is responsible for building Burj Khalifa, the tallest building in the world), he was also the biggest racehorse owner in the world. Oh, and he had just become Emir of Dubai, after his elder brother's death. I wanted so badly to beat him.

One of our trainers, Michael Jarvis, had become a genuine friend. He was another real gentleman who has unfortunately passed away since. He knew how dear was my dream of having a winning horse, and he put his heart and soul into making it happen.

Wonderful man that he was, he succeeded in training Julie's horse, Haunting Memories, to win at the August meeting in York, in front of 60,000 people. That was fantastic, but what was even better, in many ways, was that our horse beat Sheikh Mohammed Maktoum's horse into second place. The sheikh, gracious man that he was, approached us afterwards. This was a full-on sheikh, dark-eyed and handsome, with flowing robes, multiple wives, 23 children, the world's third-largest yacht, and untold millions in the bank. He was not only one of the kingpins of the United Arab Emirates from its inception in 1971, but also a superb equestrian, a generous humanitarian and social reformer, and even a well-received poet in both Arabic and Bedouin. He shook each of us by the hand and humbly wished us well for beating one of his best horses. I got a huge sense of achievement; it really was a fantasy come true.

And, just as when Marks & Spencer's management told me, "We're now making you the youngest ever buyer," the dream was over. I went on to sell the race horses soon after.

I wanted to find even more novel ways of giving back. I dreamed of an adventure that would be really tough and truly rewarding, while raising money for charity. I'd heard about Eco-Challenge: The Expedition Race, a televised, multi-day expedition-length adventure race held in different parts of the world each year. Teams of four compete, travelling non-stop for several days across different, challenging terrains. People end up in hospital. People die. It sounded perfect! I decided to do something similar, and raise money for charity. I put together my own

Eco-Challenge with a group of four compadres from Sheffield; we called ourselves the Five Men Standing. We set off on the challenge of going coast to coast across Costa Rica in ten days without any engine power. We were fortunate enough to persuade the captain of the Costa Rican Eco-Challenge team, Maurizio, to put together a route for us so that we actually had a chance of getting across the country and surviving the ten-day ordeal.

Five Men Standing

We started off on the Pacific side, traveling via mountain biking, running, hiking and kayaking, then switched in the last two days to rowing against strong wind as we approached the Caribbean Sea. The euphoria we felt when we achieved our mission at the end of the ten days was unrivaled. Those four guys – Peter Gaines, Mark Yardley, Mamad Salamat and Gian Bohan – will forever be friends. When we got back to Sheffield, we held a huge charity event, culminating in us raising £60,000 for cancer research in the UK.

My engine was running at full throttle. Even though my doctors had cleared me for travel, I don't think they had in mind traveling at the kind of speed I embarked upon now, as I turned my attention to racing cars. After training for a while for the Formula Palmer Audi series in Northampton, I decided to participate in the Gumball 3000, which is a notorious speed-freak rally through a different part of the world each year. It involves 120 cars, driven by a lot of wealthy, crazy people and celebrities who want to drive 3,000 miles in six days to various major cities. You drive all day and party all night. It was perfect for me.

Living life at full throttle

The first time I entered the Gumball 3000, the route was from London to the Monaco Grand Prix – via Prague, Vienna, Budapest, and then back up through Italy to the south of France, ending in Monte

Carlo in time for the Grand Prix. The race really reflected my passions. It consisted of illegal street racing, doing crazy things to get ahead of the other racers and avoid the police, partying at night, and being with a group of all-out speed-freak guys.

I met so many fun people, not least the guys from the MTV reality show and subsequent film, Jackass, including Johnny Knoxville, as well as Matt Pritchard, who ran the equivalent MTV show in Britain, *Dirty Sanchez*, who was Welsh, and even wilder.

My nature led me to compete with them over who would achieve the most outrageous stunts. The relationships got even more intense in the following year's Gumball 3000, which was the biggest event they have ever held with crowds of hundreds of thousands of people and an insane route.

It went from London to Prague, then Prague to Bucharest. We were plagued by rain, making crashes a more-than-likely hazard. Some of them were terrible; I witnessed a Phantom Rolls Royce lose control, spinning round and round and hitting barrier after barrier, getting smashed to pieces. Thank goodness the guys inside came out totally unharmed.

One of my more thrilling adventures was the time we were pulled over for speeding by the Austrian police near the border with Romania. Because they took their time getting out of the vehicle, my co-driver Anthony Hinchliffe decided it would be a good idea to drive off as soon as they got out of their car. The Austrian police dress in very pompous uniforms, all gold-brocade caps and flashy epaulets, meant to impress. You should have seen their faces when, instead of obediently waiting for them to come and arrest us, we hared off. We embarked on a white-knuckle race to the border, chased by the Austrian police all the way, and made it just in time to get through customs, so they couldn't catch us. It was a lot of fun!

When we got to Bucharest, Maximilian Cooper, who owned the Gumball 3000, had hired three Russian Antonov planes to put 40 cars on each and fly them to Phuket in Thailand, as well as a private plane for all the drivers. When we got to the "land of smiles," we stayed at the Amanpuri in Phuket, which had just been voted the best hotel in the world.

You can only imagine what kind of trouble 120 crazy guys got into in Phuket. One of my personal highlights was showing off to the Jackass guys and diving into a six-foot pool from a 40-foot-high house roof. Thankfully, I lived to tell the tale. None of the Jackass lads would do it, which made me quite happy.

Then, we raced from Phuket to Bangkok, the capital of Thailand, which was, hands down, the most insane ride of my life. It was like being inside a Play Station game, with vehicles traveling at huge speeds and dogs, cats, cows, children, and everything in between thrown in my direction. It was a struggle to avoid them, which I knew I must do at all costs.

Somehow, we managed to win that leg of the race and were the first to arrive at the Oriental Hotel in Bangkok. Bangkok is famous for many things, one being their tuk-tuks – three-wheeled motor bikes that are the preferred form of taxi in Bangkok's insane traffic, some of the worst in the world. Many of the Gumballers gambled with each other, offering their drivers large amounts of money to win races from one place to another. Of course, I had to take it one stage further, and convinced our Thai driver to swap places with me, so that I became the driver!

We then put the cars back onto the Antonov planes and flew to Salt Lake City in the US. With all the partying and the time differences, I don't think anybody knew what day it was or where we were. From Salt Lake City, we raced to Las Vegas and partied with Snoop Dogg, which was insane.

Next, we raced to Rodeo Drive in Beverly Hills, which had been closed down for the finish of the race. That evening, we celebrated at the final party in the Playboy mansion. To say that that was the most boring party of the seven nights gives you some insight into what the previous parties were like. I looked forward to the Gumball each year; it helped replace a lot of adrenaline I'd lost from not being in business.

Soon after, *Robb Report* magazine, chronicle of all things exciting and expensive in the world, was holding the Car of the Year Award in Napa Valley, California, and invited me to drive a wonderful range of new, upmarket demo cars, and to vote on which ones were best or worst.

The roads were closed for the event, and it was an exhilarating time, to say the least. I was awarded a beautiful piece of crystal for being the most fun participant. John Varvatos, the trendiest men's outfitter in the US, was also invited, and we hit it off straight away. I have never been one for dressing up, and he took upon himself to give me a full makeover. A new Lawrence was born, all filmed by Robb Report for their website. I have not looked back since!!

Perhaps my ultimate sporting achievement was not actually mine; it was seeing my daughter, Hannah, use her God-given athletic talents to achieve wonderful sporting success. I never missed seeing her represent Sheffield in netball and field hockey, Yorkshire at badminton and rounders, and England at rounders, as captain. Those were my proudest moments. I spent hours helping her improve at each sport, because I had hours to spend. However, badminton was the one sport where she actually beat me, and I haven't picked up a racket since!

My time off also gave me a chance to practice sports with Toby. His dream was to play for the school football team, but his asthma was prohibiting him. Night after night after school, we went to a local park. I put him in goal and taught him all I knew about goal-keeping. His determination paid off, and it made my year when Toby was chosen to be the goalkeeper for Abbey Lane Junior Football Club in Sheffield, who were at the top of their division that year.

We had a little extra help, to be honest. Matt Duke, goalkeeper for Burton Albion FC, a professional association football club based in Burton upon Trent, was a friend of mine, and he responded brilliantly to my pleas for advice. He was kind enough to spend a great deal of his time helping Toby learn to become a goalkeeper and achieve his dream. To thank him, I introduced him to my good friend, Adam Pearson, who had taken over the helm of the Hull City and became chairman of that club after a stint at Leeds United.

That connection worked out better than I could have hoped. Adam ended up asking Matt to be Hull City's goalkeeper. His salary went up five times, not including bonuses, which were substantial. Even better, Hull City made it to the Premier League, so Matt was really at the top of the game. He was such a nice guy; he deserved every second of it. The good consequences kept coming, too. When Matt later went to Bradford City, where he led them through to the League Cup final, he accepted Toby's proposal to make a documentary about him. This is an important story about connection, kindness and karma; sometimes it really does seem that everything comes around in circles.

There were many other highlights on my journey to complete the 101 things, and I'm so glad to have had the support of my wife and kids to make it happen. I spent a lot of time away from home travelling, but when Hannah and Toby were born, I made a promise to speak to them every day, regardless of where I was in the world. I kept that promise, throughout my quest. The funny thing was, so often when I called, the kids said, "Dad, please come home. Mom's got all her friends around and this party's going on; we can't sleep! We can hear the noise coming from downstairs."

I'm delighted to say that my wife enjoyed herself even when she wasn't with me, and she and the kids got to go on many adventures with me as well. There are too many incredible memories to mention, but here are some of the other things that were on the list:

- Scuba-diving with sharks and feeding them in Moorea, French Polynesia;
- Catching a fish with my bare hands in Rangiora, French Polynesia;
- Landing on Tutankhamun's tomb in Egypt by accident in a hot air balloon;
- Sky-diving from 15,000 feet in New Zealand;
- River boarding in Queenstown;
- Crowd-surfing at Stagecoach Music Festival in the US;
- Firing an AK-47 in Cambodia;
- Flying a personal rocket in Queenstown;
- Heli-biking in Queenstown;
- Blowing up a taxi in Las Vegas;
- Driving coast-to-coast from Los Angeles to Miami in the Gumball Rally;
- Playing tennis with the Old Masters of Tennis at various charity events – Boris Becker, Pat Cash, Ilie Nastase, Jimmy Connors, John McEnroe, Ivan Lendl and more;
- Playing golf with the Old Masters of Golf at various charity events – Ernie Els, Mark O'Meara, Lee Trevino, and more;
- Seeing the space shuttle launch in Florida;
- Bungee jumping in Australia;
- Experiencing zero gravity in a specialized plane in Florida;
- Getting a hole in one at golf. Twice;
- Making a fire without matches in Costa Rica;
- Going on an amazing safari to see the Big Five, and helping the local village with charity aid;
- Watching Lennox Lewis beat Mike Tyson at a World Championship boxing match in Memphis, Tennessee;
- Watching England play Brazil in the World Cup, in Japan;
- Mountain biking coast-to-coast in the UK;

- Living in the US for a period;
- Joining the mile high club; although it's a secret when that was achieved!!!
- Going into a busy bar in San Francisco and spontaneously buying everyone in the bar a drink, just because;
- Saving a baby from drowning in Sardinia;
- Learning to captain a boat and take it across the Mediterranean;
- Spending Christmas on the beach;
- Visiting the world's tallest buildings;
- Competing in triathlons;
- Renewing my wedding vows with Julie, the love of my life;
- Spending time with the Los Angeles Police Department – both on the ground in bullet-proof vests in South Central LA, and overnight in a series of helicopters, monitoring the whole city's crime spread out below.

I still have 2 of the 101 things left to do. One is to write a best-seller, which you are, I hope, holding in your hands. Number two is to live to 100; this is the least likely!!

Everyone, including me, was happy that I was finding purpose in my life and getting to experience so many great things after being so close to death while, at the same time, helping others less fortunate than myself. Altogether, counting money of my own that I donated and money I have raised, £25 million has been given to charities so far. I hope to contribute a lot more in the future.

With all of this excitement and good deeds, you'd think there was no time to fret about missing work. But a leopard doesn't change its spots, and waiting in the wings was a trusted friend with an offer I couldn't resist. In the meantime, Julie and I decided to pursue the biggest dream there is: The American Dream.

CHAPTER 9

CHASING THE AMERICAN DREAM

Julie and I had already spent enough time in America to know that we loved it and wanted to live there for a while. For me, the American Dream is a very potent one. As I've said before, I think most great business ideas come out of the minds of American entrepreneurs, and there's a freedom and sense of enthusiasm there that resonates deeply with me. I know a lot of Brits feel this way. We bring an enormous weight of tradition to what we do, which can be useful when it's business as usual, like building infrastructure projects – you still can't beat a Scottish engineer! But the rugged individualism cherished in America encourages the attitude that anything might be possible – raising cities from the desert, building skyscrapers thousands of feet tall, blasting a railway through the Rockies, putting electric light in every home. Brits spend a lot of time sneering at the fact that most Americans fail to understand our particularly dense brand of irony and talk loudly in restaurants, but the truth is that most of us secretly envy the American spirit. There was a period in the 90s when just about every heartwarming British comedy ended with a sequence in which the hero or heroine, or both, ended up in America – most often driving down that palm tree–lined stretch of Beverly Drive near Hollywood in an open-top car – fully realized as joyful human beings at last. It's a cliché, but it runs deep. Brits generally feel much more self-empowered and liberated in America. And I was no exception. Furthermore, there was a practical reason. After the terrifying medical mistakes made in the UK when treating my heart attack and its aftermath, we felt the healthcare in the US was far superior, and that my overall health would be in better hands there. We planned to decamp there by the end of the summer, 2007.

But meanwhile, there was an important goal to check off the list from "The Full Monty, 101 Things To Do Before I Die". I longed to buy a boat and travel on it throughout the Mediterranean.

So, at the end of March 2007, Julie and I took the children out of school, and the four of us departed on one of our greatest adventures. It was our goodbye to living in the UK.

We bought a 72-foot Sunseeker yacht and called it *Me Julie*. It was named after Julie, as well as the famous British TV comedian, Ali G, whose girlfriend was called "Me Julie." At the time, we had no idea that our choice of names would make the yacht a tourist attraction wherever it was docked. Everybody wanted to take a photo next to *Me Julie* because of its famous namesake.

Our home on the water

Me Julie's home port was Puerto Portals, on the island of Mallorca, but since we were on the move for the majority of our four months at sea, it spent little time there. We spent our first week in Puerto Portals, before setting sail for Ibiza, which was known as the nightlife party capital of Europe. Although Hannah and Toby were still young, we were liberal parents who allowed them to party with us. After late nights in the clubs, we spent our days relaxing on the beautiful beaches on the island of Formentera, which is opposite Ibiza. Then we returned to Mallorca.

During our glorious summer of sailing, visits from friends and family were frequent, and fun. My beloved mum came for a week with her dear friends Michael and Hazel. Mum was very shaky due to all the drugs she took for her mental health issues, and her arm movements were strange, as if she had Parkinson's, although she didn't. She rallied beautifully and enjoyed everything the boat had to offer. I loved her dearly, and it was amazing to have the chance to spend time doing something with her that brought her joy. Her visit, on its own, made the whole boating experience worthwhile.

Other visits were a great deal more raucous, for example when friends Anthony, Tim, Ian, and John came aboard *Me Julie*. They are all close compadres and memorable characters, to boot. Anthony was nicknamed "Lamppost," because he was so tall and skinny. We called Tim the rock garden, because his girlfriend once said that everything's there in perfect formation, but it's all miniature! Ian Cleeton is the funniest and scruffiest person I've ever met, and yet he went around trying to convince everyone he met that he was an around-the-world yachtsman. In reality, his yachting skills could barely get him out of the harbour, as proven when, one night, he managed to sink *Me Julie's* tender by forgetting to put the plugs in, costing me £15,000! And John (John Pemberton) was an ex-footballer who told all the girls that he used to play for Leeds United. I pointed out to him that, basically, all that meant was he was a failed footballer, but he was sufficiently successful with the lassies that he didn't seem to mind.

Their visit was a memorable round of unbridled fun. One night, when we were in a nightclub, I heard each and every one of my guests telling different girls about the wonderful 72-foot boat in the marina that he owned. It was, of course, a great chat-up line, but I didn't realize I had so many partners in my boat!! Cleeton bragged about his warehouse in Chesterfield and particularly his advanced CCTV system – which ironically was the same CCTV that the police used as evidence in his counterfeit goods trial, years later.

After all our visitors had departed and we'd seen all the sights in Mallorca, we set sail to Menorca, which was about 12 hours away. For 11 1/2 of those 12 hours, all we saw was ocean; it was a surreal feeling. Menorca was just a stopping-off point on our way to Sardinia.

After some time seeing the sights in Sardinia, we got off the boat and went to the Forte Village, which was a complex in the south of the island. For Julie and me, this is a very special place. When we first went there, at 17, we didn't have much money, and Forte Village was a cheap option. But it was and is captivating, and we completely fell in love with the place. To be honest, I think it's probably the place Julie and I fell fully in love with one another. After the kids were born, we went back again and again, and we had many wonderful family holidays there. It really was our place. It had everything, including a Chelsea Football Academy, where kids can learn from former Chelsea players. The kids got to learn to do all sorts of water sports, go-kart racing, ten-pin bowling, and, of course, football.

There were plenty of ad hoc football games with "national" teams, and we managed to put together a UK team that was the same most summers. We had me in goal; Vinnie Jones, former midfielder for Leeds United and Chelsea, now all-around hard man and Hollywood actor, in defense; Ainsley Harriott, the TV chef, and Tony Allan from the Fish! chain of restaurants in midfield; and Brian McFadden, the lead singer from the band Westlife, up front. It really felt like we were representing our country, and we rarely lost; we had great team spirit.

One thing I can tell you from all our nights of partying is that Vinnie Jones is a great singer, better than Brian McFadden, who was paid to sing. Vinnie became a good friend. Despite his reputation as a tough guy, he is a wonderful family man. When surrounded by family, he could not be any calmer and nicer.

Vinnie Jones and Toby at his side

From Sardinia, we sailed along the Amalfi Coast of Italy and then on to Croatia and Montenegro, which were our favourite places on the whole trip. It was wonderful to have Hannah and Toby to ourselves, building on the closeness we shared with our kids since the day they were born. They both slept in our bed until the age of five. Although enduring many sleepless nights for five years was difficult, every second was worthwhile because of the tight bonds that we developed as a family.

Julie is a fantastic mother. Since day one, the kids have told her everything about their lives with total openness. They know they can trust her with the mistakes they've made, and that she will always be there for them. They've benefited from having someone to speak with, someone they know won't turn on them, and it's given them so much confidence.

It wasn't all fun and games, however. In July, from the boat, I took a call from an administrator who had been appointed to deal with the administration of my old company, Out of Town Restaurants, which I had sold four years earlier. The new owners had run it into the ground and it was now in bankruptcy.

It saddened me that such a good company had gotten itself into trouble. It always amazes me when new management teams come in, thinking they know better, and start changing a well-oiled machine, only to find out that maybe the old way was better. The administrator asked me if I would buy the company back, since all the remaining senior staff made it clear that they were desperate to work with me again. But I was about to emigrate to the US.

It was James Burdall, the old friend who helped me recover after my heart attack, who persuaded me to buy back the company. I trusted him implicitly. He'd helped me through the heart attack; he was there for my first walk and my first bike ride after it. Now, he was trustee on my will, had my power of attorney, and was overseeing Bradwell's Ice Cream, too. James and I discussed the deal at length by telephone, while I was on the boat. I was still under doctor's orders to take on no business duties, so the only way we could make it work is if he managed the whole thing. He leapt enthusiastically at the opportunity to take on Out of Town Restaurants.

I trusted him, so I went through with the deal. Of course, I never expected he had any ulterior motives in encouraging me to make the purchase. But I must admit, knowing that I was emigrating to the US made the deal feel very strange. Still, I signed the documents anyway, and turned to focusing my attention on our move to Florida.

Moving from the UK to the US is much more complicated and difficult than many people would think. When we decided to make the move, we found a lawyer in London who explained the many complications we would face. He said that the best way to get a resident's visa was to take a business that we owned and put together a business plan to expand it into the US.

So we opted to create a plan to take Bradwell's Ice Cream across the Atlantic. After a whole lot of work, we were granted a one-year business visa. Once the visa side of the move was sorted out, we placed Hannah and Toby at the American school in London, so they could take the exams they would need to attend American schools. After they passed their exams, we enrolled them in the Orlando school we had already selected.

We arrived in Florida in August of 2007, just in time for the beginning of the school year. I had already visited in March 2007 and, against my better judgment, decided to buy a large house in a gated community called Isleworth, about 20 miles West of Orlando, in Florida. It had been designed by someone who had gotten himself into difficulty building "the ultimate house" in Florida. He ran out of money before he could complete it, but lucky for us, it was an incredible house.

When we arrived in August, I felt like I was seeing it for the first time, since there had been no furniture when we bought it months earlier. I had a particularly emotional moment when I saw Hannah's room – a sea of pink, with wallpaper matching the bedding – designed just the way I knew she'd love. Tears sprang from my eyes. Somehow, in that moment, I realized that I was really here. I was alive. I was with my family. After a year of recuperation, I could rely more on my health. I had survived the heart attack, and I felt my life moving forward would be a good one.

In the beginning, being in a new country was tough for the kids. They had left behind all their friends and the way of life they knew. But within a month, both Hannah and Toby loved it. Kids are amazingly adaptable. They were both well-liked and had extra social standing because they were from England. Within a couple of months, also, Julie had befriended some fun ladies who lived inside Isleworth. So she was really happy. Another box had been ticked off.

The lawyer who helped us get our business visa had pointed out that there was something called an EB-1 specialist visa. The lawyer felt that, with my track record, I could be eligible for this visa because it was reserved for people who are recognized as being at the very top of their field and who are coming to the United States to continue work in that field. The EB stands for "extraordinary ability"; it's for people who've won the Nobel Prize and the like. I thought he was joking! But I applied, and three months later, a green card arrived for Julie, Hannah, Toby, and me – another box ticked.

Isleworth bills itself as "one of the most prestigious private golf club communities in the world, featuring championship golf and a collection of amenities paired with extraordinary estate homes." In other words, it's a golf course with homes around it. I realized that if I wanted to make friends, I'd have to take up golf. And I would have to get good at it, too, fast. Tiger Woods was a neighbour, for one, along with loads of other famous people from various walks of life, all of whom seemed to love to play golf all day long. I'd played a tiny bit in England, but not much. I'd never taken the game seriously, and I found it a bit boring. Honestly, I still do, but I made learning it a priority, nonetheless.

My investment paid off. Through golf, I met a guy called Bing Kearney. Bing was a redneck who had done well as a property developer. He had his own Gulfstream jet, yet he had never been outside the United States. He took a liking to me and introduced me to a group of guys in Tampa, about an hour away from Orlando, who ended up becoming really good friends. Six months after moving to America, Bing invited me to Sage Valley, near Augusta, Georgia, where they hold the Masters, the biggest golf tournament in the world.

On the first night, Bing turned to me and said, "I've got something very special for you tomorrow."

Watching the Masters at Augusta was every golfer's dream. But that wasn't enough for Bing – he'd arranged for me to actually play there!

All of a sudden, only six months after taking up golf seriously, I was living the fantasy of golfers everywhere. Not surprisingly, I struggled through the main course, but they have a par three course, where most of the participants play every Wednesday before the Masters, and where I could practise. Most of these consummate professionals don't actually shoot par on this course; they'll be two or three over. But I actually managed to shoot an even par, a minor miracle I felt sure would never be achieved again. That was my first big achievement in golf, and I have to say, the game began to grow on me.

Living in an American gated community for the super-wealthy felt a bit weird at times. But it did put me in contact with some pretty extraordinary people. Sammy Duvall, who used to be a world champion waterskier, taught me how to wake-surf, where you trail behind a boat on a surf board, riding the boat's wake without being directly pulled by the boat. He showed me lots of tricks and skills. I could play a game of basketball with Shaq O'Neal in the indoor court inside Champion's Grill at the clubhouse. Or I'd be off playing golf, and Tiger Woods, the best golfer the world had ever seen, would be making fun of my golf swing. Mind you, I can't exactly hold that against him!

I had an interesting relationship with Tiger. Julie and I became friends with his wife, and I certainly didn't like what he did to her, which was only revealed later, when the scandal broke about his adultery. But that wasn't the source of the tension in 2007. Like most famous people, he had a lot of people sucking up to him. As a Sheffield guy, I was not interested in sucking up to anyone, and he didn't particularly like that.

With Tiger Woods on the golf course

My early success at golf encouraged me to enter a competition called the Outback Steakhouse Pro-Am, which was on the senior tour with professional players over the age of 50. As an amateur, I got to play with world-class players, in a competition in front of 15,000 people.

At the time I didn't know it, but the guy responsible for this, Chris Sullivan from Tampa, had set up the Outback chain of restaurants, as well as Bonefish, Fleming's, and other chains. He loved golf and had his own private golf course. Since I did so well during the three-day competition, I got to play in the final group with him and Tom Watson, a very famous golfer, live on television.

Halfway through the round, I hit a bad shot. Julie and the kids were following me, and they overheard one spectator turn to her husband and say, "Even you're better than that!" Luckily, I didn't hear, and I wouldn't have cared anyway. But later that day, something happened that had the potential to be a serious problem. Luckily, it ended up being funny. After a shot, there was a question about whether my ball was out of bounds.

An official had to be called. It took a long time. Eventually, I hit the ball over a hill to a destination unseen on the other side. Unbeknownst to me, Tom Watson was playing right in its path. It whistled past his head, missing him by inches. I could have brained the man who consistently beat Jack Nicklaus! Now that would have made the headlines.

Isleworth had a member guest golf tournament each year. I always invited my best friend, Nidge from Sheffield, to be my partner. Craig Johnstone, a former striker for Liverpool and the first Australian to make his mark on English and European football, was a fellow resident of Isleworth. He was dating Vivian Lewis, the daughter of Joe Lewis, who owns Isleworth Golf and Country Club, along with another 170 companies around the world. Each year, Craig invited Kenny Dalglish and Alan Hansen for a visit. Nidge and I became friends with them both.

We used to go out to dinner and have singing competitions. They sang Liverpool songs and we sang Sheffield United songs. One night, Nidge had too much to drink. He went out on the terrace for a cigarette and fell asleep. Kenny went to the bar, filled a bucket with ice and water, went outside and poured it on Nidge's head. Nidge woke up with a terrible shock, and I saw the red mist come down. He was moments away from knocking King Kenny's head off. I jumped in and somehow managed to calm him down.

Mick McCliman, the best knee surgeon in Tampa, became a dear friend. Each year, he organized the McCliman's Clambake. Sounds like a non-golf event, right? Actually, it included a three-day golfing tournament. The idea of the tournament was that it gave you a chance to pay respects to the person who introduced you to golf, all the while competing for a good-sized pot of money.

Through golf, I also met Mickey Carney, who, over the years, has become a close friend. We have gone on to win many golf competitions together at various clubs, most notably, Bay Hill, where we were the only pair to ever win back-to-back member guest tournaments there. As the third year's tournament approached, I asked Arnold Palmer what would happen if we won three in a row. He shrugged his shoulders and replied flatly, "You won't." As usual, he was right. We came DFL: dead flipping last!!

Making friends with all these guys in Tampa was something that I never expected in this second stage of my life. I felt so welcome, so loved, in the same way I did with my best friends from Sheffield that I've known since birth. I wanted to pay the guys back for being so kind to me and helping me settle into Florida.

So I organized a ten-day trip for 16 of us to all the best golf courses in Scotland. It always amazes me how few Americans have ever left the country – fully 12 of them had to get passports for the trip. I rented out whole castles like Culzean, which was designed by the amazing 18th-century neoclassical architect Robert Adam. My friend who owns The Ashvale Fish Restaurant in Aberdeen, the best fish and chip restaurant in the UK, organized a full whisky tour one night. Everyone had the best trip of their lives, and it gave me so much joy to see the guys have new experiences and so much fun.

My friendships with John Noriega, Alan Payne, Bing Kearney, Mikey Carney, Paul O'Renick, Mickey Carney, Dave Donoho and Clif Curry were sealed forever, and we still keep in contact with each other regularly.

I seem to have talents as a travel agent. A couple of years later, I organized a similar trip to Ireland, then one to England, and finally one to New Zealand. Some, if not all, of the guys that went to Scotland came on those trips as well, and everybody said they had the most amazing time of their lives.

I cast myself as a reluctant golfer, but I can't complain. I've played on some of the most gorgeous golf courses in the world, including Royal

County Downs, Ireland; Augusta, Georgia; Pine Valley, Pennsylvania; Cypress Point, California; and Shinnecock Hills, Long Island.

Through the Isleworth grapevine I heard that, for whatever reason, Joe Lewis, who owns Isleworth Golf and Country Club and much else besides, wanted to meet me. Forbes says he's worth $8 billion. He's worth a lot more than that; he's one of the wealthiest people in the world. I assume he wanted to meet me because I was a new owner of a big property in his community. But whatever was the reason, we got on like a house on fire. Speaking of fire, the first time I visited his house was a blistering Orlando summer day. I was shocked when I walked into his living room and saw that the fire was on.

"Why on earth would you be sitting here with the fire turned on during this blazing hot day?" I asked.

"Go over and put your hand in it," he directed me.

I thought he was joking and did not take him up on his offer. So he demonstrated for me himself. He walked up, put his hand right in the flames, and smiled. It was an illusion, just part of his amazing art collection, one of the best in the world. Joe was great to Julie and me. The relationship blossomed, and it eventually led to us moving to Albany, his development in the Bahamas.

At this point, the kids were now ready to graduate from school. We looked at many universities, most of them local to Florida and the East Coast. But both of them decided to go and live in California. Hannah fell in love with University of Southern California (USC) in Los Angeles. Toby, also, with his dream firmly set on a career in film, did not want to be far away from the heartbeat of the film industry in Los Angeles. He applied to USC and the Dodge Film School at Chapman, and was admitted to both, but chose Chapman because of the collaborative atmosphere they promoted, as opposed to the dog-eat-dog attitude at USC.

Julie and I faced an empty nest, but we were so well integrated at Isleworth, we weren't especially worried. But just as the kids were departing for their universities in California, the US government made some decisions that made us question staying in our new-found home.

CHAPTER 10

THE AMERICAN DREAM OVER AND MOVING ON

While we were enjoying our life in Florida and building all kinds of new relationships, the US government stupidly changed its rules on green card holders. They decided two things. One, if you are a green card holder but not a citizen and you pass away, the death duty is much higher than for US citizens. Not only is the threshold for tax exclusion on money transferred after death only 35 percent of $60,000 (instead of 35 percent of $5 million for US citizens), the marital deduction extended to US citizens (an exemption for assets transferred to your spouse) does not apply to green card holders either. Two, if you hold a US green card for 8 out of 15 years, when you leave, you have to pay an "exit tax" that treats all your assets as having been liquidated and subject to tax at an exorbitantly high rate.

Ironically, the changes came under what was known as The HEART Act – H.R. 6081 – 110th Congress: Heroes Earnings Assistance and Relief Tax Act of 2008 – passed on 17 June 2008. It was a fairly typical piece of badly thought-out US legislation, presented as an amendment to the Internal Revenue Code of 1986, in order to "provide benefits for military personnel, and for other purposes". Ridiculously, it tried to fund improvements in benefits for US military personnel by gouging non-US citizens! Well, I had already had one heart attack. These new rules were nothing short of daylight robbery. Since we had never earned a penny in the US, we certainly were not going to pay this money in either event. One of my friends was good friends with then-Florida governor Jeb Bush, and because he was so upset with these decisions from the US government, he took it up with Jeb directly. Jeb looked into it and explained that, as with any government, the left arm did not know what the right arm was doing, and different departments had made different decisions, which all added up to a political shambles.

For Julie and me, this explanation wasn't good enough. As soon as the kids left for their respective universities, we moved to the Bahamas. When we got there, we took the very unusual step of handing back our green cards at the US Embassy in Nassau. The embassy staff could not believe that we were doing this. Three times, they asked us if we were sure we wanted to do it. They actually made us go back the next day after we had had time to think about it. But our decision was made. We became Bahamian residents.

It astonishes me how the United States can allow people to enter the country on a massive basis who frequently use and abuse healthcare, schools, and other benefits while making little or no contribution to the country. Yet here we were, a couple, with two children living in the United States, who were contributing charitably, financially, and in plenty of other ways to the country, and yet we were forced out by punitive tax laws. We were surprised, disappointed and angry.

The United States is the only country in the world, other than Eritrea, that taxes its citizens on any income earned anywhere in the world. And Eritrea charges its citizens only 2 percent, compared to the US top tax rate of nearly 40 percent. Even the UN Security Council condemned Eritrea for "using extortion, threats of violence, fraud and other illicit means to collect taxes outside of Eritrea from its nationals." (It has remained silent on the extortionate US tax laws.) All other countries welcome anybody who purchases a property and comes in with a net wealth of a certain value attained by legal means. The United States should greet such people with open arms and instant green cards. I feel it is completely counter-productive for them to make it so challenging to become part of their great country.

As I mentioned before, Joe Lewis counted among his many assets Albany, the brand-new development in the Bahamas where we chose to live. What a gorgeous place it is! Tucked away on the southwest side of the island of New Providence, it's a luxury resort community set on 600 ocean-side acres, with an 18-hole golf course designed by Ernie Els, who is an investor, as is Tiger Woods. The name Albany comes from its centerpiece Albany House, a pink beachfront Bahamian manor house with an on-screen credit as the home of the villain in the Bond film Casino Royale. Needless to say, it has a colossal marina and multiple swimming pools, spa, gym, restaurants, and everything else you could want in such a location.

Joe was kind enough to sit down with Julie and me to explain how to make the most of being in the Bahamas. He told us that it was the best boating spot in the world. He, for example, lives permanently on his 280-foot boat anchored in the Albany marina, so he knows better than anybody. He said one of the main things to do in the Bahamas was enjoy the waters. He was so right. We had a lot of fun exploring all things aquatic, and we bought another boat. This one was a 55-foot yacht, and, drawing on our experience in the Med, Julie and I decided to skipper it ourselves. We had so many happy and funny times, but some scary ones as well. On one trip, we foolishly tied our tender to a dock on one of Bahamas' 700 islands without considering the movement of the tides. Oblivious, we went off to drink and eat at a local bar. When we returned, definitely the worse for wear, the tide had gone down, leaving the tender hanging vertically from its rope, mostly in the air and with only its very tip in the sea. We were drunk and didn't know what to do.

The first thing we tried to do was sleep on the sand by the dock, but the mosquitos were eating us alive. In the end, we managed to get more rope to lower the boat down and eventually get it loose. Thank God, somebody was watching us do all this, even though it was two in the morning.

In our drunken state, we used the tender's engine to take us back to our boat, further out in the sea. As Julie tried to jump from the tender onto the boat, she fell in, and was only just clinging to the side of our yacht. The current was very strong, and I knew if she let go of the boat she was gone for good. So I managed to tie the tender off, and jumped onto the boat so I could get a good grip on her. But when Julie took my hand, she yanked me hard enough to pull me in as well. Now, we were both in a very dangerous position. Whoever had been watching us from the shore saw what was happening and helped us back onto the boat. Without him, we would have been in deep trouble.

Another time, we broke down in the middle of the sea with no telephone signal and no engine power. For a long period of time, the waves just moved us around. It took me two hours in a burning-hot engine room to figure out how to get the boat restarted.

But mostly, we just had fun. We had wonderful times swimming with the now-famous swimming pigs in the Exumas, in the Thunderball Cave where the James Bond film was made. We hung out with the nurse sharks in Compass Cay. They look like sharks, but are actually huge catfish, and swim up to you and seem to enjoy having their photos taken. We had fun times in the Abacos group of islands, only 190 miles off the coast of Florida, particularly at Bakers Bay, another sumptuous community with a Tom Fazio–designed oceanfront golf course. These are memories that will live with me forever.

Of course, I was still on my mission to complete my "Full Monty". One of my dreams that came true in the Bahamas was an equestrian one. I'd always dreamed of riding a horse, but unfortunately I'm allergic to horses. I found this out the hard way, when I was four and my dad took me to a circus in Sheffield. Half-way through the performance, I collapsed with breathing trouble and was rushed to hospital. It turns out I have a very strong allergy to horses, which I like to joke is at its most potent when I gamble on them and they lose! When the horses were winning all those races in England, I had to stay a long way away in the stands; it was always up to Julie and the kids to collect our trophies.

But I always dreamed of riding a horse, just once. At Albany, there were horses that loved to ride along the beach and in the sea. I had watched them from afar with longing; they looked so wild and free. The wonderful staff at Albany arranged a wetsuit, booties, gloves, and a ride on one of those horses. I looked absolutely ridiculous. In addition to all the neoprene, I was wearing a snorkel and mask! I'm sure everybody that saw me thought it was hilarious. But for one hour, I was able to live my dream without any adverse reaction.

To add to the joy of the Bahamas, Joe Lewis explained how we could make the most of the tax system there, which I love. There's VAT of 7.5 percent which, when added to the high cost of importing everything onto an island, makes everything very expensive. The government has to raise money from somewhere, so that comes from placing duty on everything that comes into the country. But there's no income tax, no capital gains tax, and no death tax. Property tax is 1% on property valued up to $500,000, and is only 2% above that. Mostly what appeals is that everybody, no matter what their level of income, gets to keep virtually all their money. The people decide what to spend money on, rather than handing 30% or 40% of it over to the government.

Heeding Joe's advice, we moved everything to the Bahamas: our home, all our possessions, our investment companies, our wills, our trusts, our club membership, our driving licenses, our residence. We even chose and purchased our burial sites there. We committed to the Bahamas 100% and became officially domiciled there. We planned to spend the rest of our lives there. We played golf with the likes of Adam Scott, Ian Poulter, Justin Rose, and Ernie Els, who were all fellow residents. We played tennis with Ivan Lendl and Jim Courier among others.

Tiger Woods also had a connection to the Bahamas, as an investor in the Albany community. Tiger's main passion is free diving, and he has got down to 108 feet. Albany was perfect for him, as there were no prying eyes and no one to bother him, so he could actually relax there.

In later years, when life has not been as good for him, things have been better between us. I spent time with him recently in Vegas, and he was much friendlier than previously. I believed then and I believe now that he wasted a resource that was just around the corner, but he didn't take advantage of it. My feeling is that he could have received much useful advice and help from Arnold Palmer, the Old Master of Golf, who owned the golf club next to Isleworth when Tiger lived there. I think he would have helped Tiger better manage and restore his life and reputation. Mr. Palmer was in many ways the opposite from Tiger: a complete gentleman and a fully developed person whom everybody loved. He would walk up and shake anyone's hand and was always ready to pose for pictures with his fans. I actually told Tiger, "If I were you, I'd just go and spend a month with Arnold and learn from the master himself."

While we were having such a great time in the Bahamas, we were seven hours away from the two things we loved most of all: Hannah and Toby. This became unbearable. We searched for a location where we could all conveniently meet for a few days' holiday, and lighted upon Cabo San Lucas, on the west coast of Mexico. We fell in love with a development there called El Dorado, and decided to buy a casita there so we could spend part of the year closer to the children. El Dorado is a stunning, exclusive, gated golf and beach club community with over one mile of stunning coastline along the Sea of Cortez, full of beautiful, custom-made homes and yet another celebrity-approved 18-hole golf course, this one designed by Jack Nicklaus.

If we thought that Isleworth in Orlando was an adult Disneyland, our eyes were really opened in El Dorado. Leonardo DiCaprio lived next door. Alexander Rodriguez, the famous American baseball player otherwise known as A-Rod, and Michael Phelps, the Olympic swimmer, lived directly above us. Hank Haney, Tiger Woods' old coach, lived down the road, and we swapped many stories about Tiger. Other well-known residents included George Clooney, Cindy Crawford, and Adam Levine from the band Maroon 5, to name a few. El Dorado is tequila party central, and the resort's 90-foot boat, *El Discovery*, set the scene for some pretty wild behavior. In fact, we dubbed it *SS ShitShow* because of all the drama and adventures it hosted, populated by El Dorado's apparently endless supply of world-class characters.

The one thing that stands out above all else was the love, passion, genuineness and honesty of the local Mexican people. We fell in love with them hook, line, and sinker. Most countries on earth would be desperate to utilize the work ethic of these people and would appreciate what they are willing to give, right on their doorstep, at a rate of pay so much lower than the US, but the US does not make the most of its neighbour to the south.

Between swimming with whales, dolphins, and sea lions, incredible mountain biking in the Eastern Cape, buying a dune buggy that could achieve 70 miles an hour off-road, and parties with the stars, we had an amazing time. However, the kids had a challenge for me: I'd never learned to surf. And so, at 50, I took it on. I was canny enough to seek out someone who would be an excellent teacher and became really good friends with Izzy Paskowitz, the famous world champion surfer who had given his life over to his autistic son.

Izzy runs an amazing charity, which we support, called Surfing for Autism. He found that when he took his severely autistic son out on the surfboard, it was the only time that he could get him to calm down and relax. It turned out that surfing had the same effect on other autistic children. Having identified this special gift, he now takes it all around the world to camps for people with autistic children. It's amazing to watch the kids go into the sea screaming and come out with smiling faces.

Izzy took it upon himself to teach me to surf. I can safely say that it's the most difficult thing I have ever learned. I recently managed to surf in 20-foot waves, admittedly not having a clue what I was doing, and holding on for dear life.

In Cabo, a few people became special to me. Jimmy Burrows – who directed numerous TV shows, including *Friends, Taxi, Will & Grace,* and *The Big Bang Theory* – and his wife Debbie became good friends. We were proud to sit next to Jimmy when NBC recently recorded a two-hour special to commemorate all the shows he had put together over his lifetime. For the final part of the show, we actually held hands as tears poured down his face, which was a really special moment.

Marco Peña, head of Outdoor Pursuits (all outdoor activities), became a great friend, and we had some memorable adventures together, including trekking in the Sierra de la Laguna mountains, 7,200 feet high, and breaking the record for kayaking from El Dorado to Cabo San Lucas – a stretch of 17 gruelling miles.

Len Pagon, the bright star in the field of online marketing technology, became a good friend, and he joined the last trip I organised to New Zealand.

Even though we were committed to the Bahamas long term and had bought a casita in Cabo San Lucas, we still managed to spend time in Newport Beach to be near the children whenever it was possible. It was fantastic to see them growing up through university and into their first jobs.

For Hannah's graduation, we went to Las Vegas. I managed to get a room in the mansions, the exclusive part of the MGM Grand usually reserved for famous people or high rollers. I had booked a party table at one of Vegas's hot clubs, and it was a fantastic night, but when I woke up the following morning my trousers were soaking wet and I found a huge bill in my wallet.

My friend Mickey Carney, who was present at the celebration, came round for breakfast and showed me the videos from the night before. First, he showed me a video of beautiful girls in the nightclub presenting a big bottle of Dom Perignon champagne with fireworks coming out of it. No wonder the bill was so big! The second video was of me being escorted out of the fountain in the middle of the hotel at 4:00 a.m. That explained the wet trousers. What a night!

In California, we met some great characters, including local real estate agents Chris and Sharon Valli, who came to my fiftieth birthday. I also met Nat DiCarlo, a former financial advisor with Smith Barney, with whom I started doing business. As my health continued to improve, I wanted to do more physically. I was already getting at least two hours of serious physical exercise at least six times a week. I was a good swimmer, good on a bike, and okay at running. My next goal was to complete a triathlon. Not too many people who have had a heart attack go on to endure triathlons; that made me even more determined.

I astonished myself when I completed the Newport Beach triathlon – half a mile swim, a 15-mile bike ride and a 3-mile run – in 1 hour and 35 minutes.

I started going to Cal a Vie health resort near San Diego – the best health resort I have ever been to – and Julie and I love it there. John and Terri Havens who own it became good friends. Sarah, who works in their gym, still trains me before each triathlon.

While all this fun was going on, I knew that I had something more to add to the business world, particularly after the worldwide financial meltdown in 2008. In 2009, I called Mike Linter, a partner at KPMG in the UK, and a tax expert. I told him about my situation, and that I wanted something to do to keep my brain occupied, but didn't want hundreds of employees or to take on a huge amount of stress. A new chapter of my life was born almost instantly.

CHAPTER 11

POACHER TURNED GAMEKEEPER

At my request, Mike Linter at KPMG introduced me to Phil Lunn and Steve Redshaw of Lateral Properties, who during the recession had bought up a stretch of Parliament Street in the centre of Harrogate – an upmarket and beautiful Spa town in North Yorkshire consistently voted by property website Rightmove as "the happiest place to live" in Britain. Harrogate is a very historic city, so planning permission for any kind of expansion or change is extremely difficult to attain. Further, Phil and Steve had run out of funds. In the wake of the recent banking meltdown, banks appeared to have forgotten that their business was lending money, and getting access to capital was a huge challenge at the time. But Phil and Steve were truly onto something, and I decided to join in.

Phil and Steve had found a great deal on buying the Royal Baths building, at the bottom of Parliament Street, right at the time the financial crisis was at its peak. The asset management company wanted out, and agreed to sell the famous building at a 10 percent yield, i.e. 10 times the rent, a good deal considering that, in normal times, the building would sell at a 6 percent yield, or 16 times the rent.

The tenants were solid. They were Weatherspoon's, the UK's leading pub company; Revolution Bar, a famous nightclub; and a very successful Chinese restaurant.

Underneath was a car park that was completely under-utilized. More opportunity emerged when we did our research and found out that this huge building had not been managed at all well. Not only were we buying it very cheaply because of the financial crisis; the rent reviews had not been triggered every five years, as they should have been. The tenants in the building opposite were paying twice as much rent per square foot as the tenants in the Baths, which would be very useful evidence when we came to review the rents. So there was more growth available there as well.

It all added up to a once-in-a-lifetime deal.

I appointed my Sheffield solicitor and accountants to set up a structure and advise on the purchase of the Royal Baths.

As I settled into the idea of owning and managing a historic landmark, I began to understand Phil and Steve's business strategy better. The street they had managed to buy so much of, Parliament Street, had dazzling potential for growth. With multiple restaurants on offer at the Royal Baths at the bottom, and the world-famous Bettys Tea Rooms – the 12th most popular paid-for attraction in the UK – at the top, it had the sort of huge, guaranteed pedestrian flow a property developer could barely dream about. It wasn't as if Harrogate as a town was a high-risk bet, either, as the two other main streets in the city were very successful. Somehow, Parliament Street below Bettys had been left in the Dark Ages. That needed to change.

We came up with a plan to make this one of the main leisure destinations in the north. It was perfect, because we had fantastic contacts in the restaurant and bar business. So many of the guys we worked with when they were managers of restaurants were now directors of those businesses. Phil and Steve were commercial property experts, and they quickly got Simon and me up to speed. It was a marriage made in heaven. I was confident I could make this investment into a spectacular winner.

We started with Harrogate House, next door to the Royal Baths, another huge property. In there, we put Jamie's Italian Restaurant, part of the chain started by celebrity and tireless benefactor Jamie Oliver. On either side of Jamie's, we put The Pit, a very successful bar concept aimed at the younger crowd, as well as Nando's, the Portuguese chicken chain. We then added more bars and restaurants down the street, to where Harrogate House meets the Royal Baths

The levels of rent were the highest ever achieved in Harrogate, which only went to increase the value of the Royal Baths further. Parliament Street was now becoming the "in" place. With Wagamama, the hipster noodle chain, in place, it was time to make the next building up the street sing. In that location, we introduced All Bar One, owned by Mitchell & Butlers (in turn owned by none other than Joe Lewis); Five Guys, Marston's public house and other local bar and restaurants; as well as the obligatory coffee shop, in this case, Café Nero.

The final piece of the jigsaw was to bring the Ivy, the UK's most iconic restaurant, to the North. They chose our final building in Harrogate as the location.

The poacher had truly turned gamekeeper.

As we've met and exceeded our goals in transforming one of the UK's most historic and wealthiest cities, this project has become one of our greatest achievements, providing some of our proudest times. It encouraged us to get involved in similar projects in other UK cities, including Leeds, Darlington and Glasgow.

But the project that stands out to me is our location at Coliseum, next to Cheshire Oaks in Cheshire.

Phil and Steve were unsure about this site, which is a retail park adjacent to the largest designer outlet mall in the UK, including a cinema, bowling alley, more shops and – our target – several food retailers. Phil and Steve shared the concerns of the major property funds that there were only a few years left on the leases to KFC and TGI Fridays, meaning guaranteed revenue was limited. However, when we visited the site, our pooled decades of knowledge about the restaurant business told us that this was a very viable prospect indeed; the volume of customer visits was enormous.

We were fully aware that millions of shoppers would be spending hours trawling the quarter-million square feet of retail space and more than 145 boutiques in our location next to Cheshire Oaks, and they were going to get hungry. Basically, everyone who went to the centre would have to pass our site, and we knew that KFC and TGI would be desperate to renew their leases. We also reckoned that the amount of space designated for car parking spaces was a lot more than needed. During the due diligence stage, we approached the local planners and asked if we could take some parking away and put another building on the site. They were very interested, so long as we did not touch the famous oak trees that gave Cheshire Oaks its name.

After the sale was complete, we went out to the market, and a bidding war ensued between Starbucks and Costa Coffee. Costa Coffee won and agreed to pay twice as much as KFC and TGI were paying per square foot. KFC and TGI will now have to match that rent at review. What a deal.

We began to realize just how much money we had made for our landlords when we were the tenants. Back in the 90s, for just one unit in Meadowhall's food court, in which we installed a Potato Bakehouse, we agreed a rent of £240,000 per annum for 600 square feet. That's a whopping £4,000 per square foot, which, must be some kind of record for the time.

All these property deals took us through a fantastic learning curve that would be highly useful for making deals in the future, but with the market so hot, it was time to unload and take profits. I have observed many times in business that too many people don't want to let go and then later wish they had. There's absolutely nothing wrong with taking a profit and leaving something on the table for the buyer. As I said before: good business is where everyone makes money. If you try to buy at the very bottom and sell at the very top all the time, you will come unstuck. We cashed out and made a very pretty penny indeed.

But sadly, just as I was expanding into a whole new entrepreneurial role, I was about to experience something else new and much less pleasant – the betrayal of one of my most trusted friends and colleagues. My collaboration with Phil and Steve, which brought me so much else, paid off in another way I could never have imagined, because it was they who uncovered the wrongdoings of James Burdall. My so-called friend turned out to be a fraud and a thief. I wish I'd known when James Burdall came into my life, offering so convincingly to help me in my darkest days, that he would end up wreaking more havoc than my heart attack.

As I explained before, when I moved to the US in 2007, I handed over to Burdall all operations of my remaining, active businesses in the UK – Bradwell's Ice Cream and the re-purchased Out of Town Restaurants Group. Burdall was also trustee on my will and had power of attorney over my affairs in my absence. I've always been careful to take good care of the people who look after my business, and Burdall was no exception. I treated him well, providing him with great income, incentives, and paid holidays. Clearly, this was not enough for him.

Phil and Steve caught Burdall out when, by sheer coincidence, I was visiting the UK on a two-week holiday. Burdall had called them to ask for money from the property company to put into Bradwell's Ice Cream. It made no sense to them, and they let me know. Since I was in the country, I went to meet Burdall face-to-face to discuss it with him. Sitting in a room with him, I could tell something was wrong, and pressed him. Making out like it was no particular big deal, he admitted he had borrowed some money from the company to tide him over on a couple of debts. Naturally, I wanted to know how much. He started at £10,000, but by the time I went to bed that evening, the figure was into hundreds of thousands. And by the time we looked into it the following day, the true amount was in the millions. I was completely shocked and horrified.

Once I'd gathered myself together again, I called the people I knew I could trust: Trevor, my old trusted lawyer; and Simon Heath, my long-term friend and business partner. They dropped everything and were with me that very day, so that the work of finding out what on earth was going on could begin immediately. Our very first move was to interview the company's accountant. At Burdall's urging, I had agreed to move the account away from my trusted accountant at Hart Shaw in Sheffield to Barber Harrison & Platt, where Burdall's godfather was senior partner. When we explained what James had been doing for so long, the accountant looked as if she'd seen a ghost. Whether she was in shock because she was surprised at Burdall's theft, or whether it was because she never expected him to get found out, I honestly don't know. I will never know the real truth.

It emerged that Burdall had committed several crimes against me. One, he had somehow managed to convince Meadowhall Shopping Centre to let both Out of Town Restaurants and Bradwell's Ice Cream fall behind on months and months of rent. I have never understood how he did this. Back when I was in charge, a bailiff would show up at your restaurant door the next day if you did not pay the rent on time. But for some reason, James was allowed to build up massive arrears, paying nothing while he extracted large sums from the business – all of which ended up in his pocket.

Out of Town Restaurants and Bradwell's Ice Cream were pulling in significant amounts of money during this time, and he was able to make use of this as he pleased. At the end of the year, the accountant at Barber Harrison & Platt had raised an alarm, asking James about his habit of transferring huge amounts from my companies to his accounts. Instead of alerting me to these irregularities, they advised him to pay dividends out to himself to cover the amounts and make them look legitimate, but he didn't bother to do so. Even if he had, it would not have been convincing.

The weekend he was caught and began to confess, we were all worried about the stress these events were placing on my heart. Certainly, there was no shortage of drama. When I went into the office that Sunday, I found, to my astonishment, Burdall and his wife Helen ripping out the company's computers and attempting to destroy all the evidence of their wrongdoing. I told them to stop or I would have no choice but to call the police. They just told me to "f*** off." So I called the police right away, and Burdall and his partner in crime took off. I have to take my hat off to the police, who were brilliant from the moment they arrived, and all through their three-year investigation. They raided James Burdall's house that very night and took away a huge amount of evidence with them. It became clear that they thoroughly disliked Burdall, in part because they found a great deal of disturbing material on his computer, quite aside from the information they needed for my case. I have no idea what they found, because they never shared it with me. I shudder to think what someone with Burdall's total lack of morals could have gotten himself into.

In the span of just three years, he had cost me in excess of £3 million. It was a mighty blow. It meant the demise of Out of Town Restaurants Group. It also cost me the Bradwell's Ice Cream kiosks in Meadowhall Shopping Centre, where it all began. People think so-called "white collar" crime is victimless, and I'm sure that's what Burdall thought as he dipped into the till with breathtaking boldness again and again, but nothing could be further from the truth. Out of Town Restaurants was a healthy, successful business, supporting one thousand employees and their families. The money Burdall stole – including unpaid debts and hundreds of thousands owed to landlords – left too huge a gap for me to plug. I had to let all those staff members go. He had also put Bradwell's Ice Cream, the business built by three generations of an honest family, into peril. I was heartbroken. The police only went after him for an amount that could never have been contested, which was £1.2 million in fraud. To them, it didn't really matter, as the jail sentence between £1 and £3 million is the same, at four years, and I understand. But it mattered to me.

What hurt most, when it all came out at trial, was not even the amount of money, but the fact that Burdall had transferred £20,000 on the day he took over the checkbook, the very day I left for the United States. What a complete and utter scumbag. Three years later, in his summing up before sentencing, the judge stated that Mr. Wosskow had suffered two unfortunate events in the 21st century – one, having a heart attack; and two, reacquainting himself with James Burdall from school. James was sentenced to four years in prison, and because of the fraud and the nature of what he did, the debt will live with him forever.

Burdall seems to have made life in jail far more comfortable than it should be, and there have been a number of press articles about him living it up behind bars at Hatfield Prison, having things done for him, and effectively having staff to look after him. One article in particular sickened me, along with the thousand people who lost their jobs because of his dishonesty. He was allowed out of prison on day release to run the Yorkshire Half Marathon for his pleasure, which was disgusting. One of the major newspapers in the UK actually headlined their article "On the Run."

Not only did James Burdall cost me money, he also cost me many other important assets. When I did the deal with Eddie Healey to buy Out of Town Restaurants for a pound, agreeing that he would raise the rent to £1 million a year the following year, he gave me a 25-year lease on the Bradwell's ice cream carts in Meadowhall – something he did to thank me. Normal leases were no more than a year on ice cream carts.

When the wrongdoing of James Burdall was exposed, the Trafford Centre immediately responded that they would do whatever they could to help me save the company, because we'd been such a good tenant since the Centre opened in 1998. They increased the lease by ten years and helped us in every way they could by allowing us to pay rent monthly rather than quarterly. I will be forever grateful to the Trafford Centre for what they did.

Meadowhall, now under new ownership, took a different route. They used the non-payment of rent by Burdall to evict us from the shopping center, where it all began. This was a very sad day for me and all forty staff members who lost their jobs.

I will always live in hope that one day, Bradwell's Ice Cream will be reinstated in Meadowhall, following the thousands of letters sent to both the shopping center and to us.

Meanwhile, Bradwell's, which had been with me since the beginning, was completely raided of its cash and its wealth.

As you remember, I had made a solemn promise to Noel Bradwell that I would never let his beloved company fall into anyone else's hands, and I am a man of my word. Further, I just could not allow Jane Bownes, Mark Bownes, and Simon Allott to lose their jobs. They had worked so hard for decades to make Bradwell's into a brand that would have made Noel Bradwell so proud. Therefore, I decided that I would put £500,000 of my own money into Bradwell's to make things right with all the debtors and save the company.

This started an unpleasant run for myself and Julie.

My beloved mum passed away in 2010, and I could not return back to Julie and the kids in the US after the funeral because of the eruption of the Icelandic volcano, whose plume of ash stopped all transatlantic flights for weeks. Shortly after, Julie's dad passed away. Then, the company to whom my dad had sold out his shops many years before, Cattles Holdings Finance Ltd., and in which he taken shares as payment, discovered internal fraud which destroyed the company's share value, and my dad's shareholding went from a substantial chunk of wealth to nothing practically overnight. Like they say: when it rains it pours!!

But a bad run always calls for a new beginning. I wanted to move onwards and upwards. It was time to take what we had learnt in the UK commercial property market, as well as the resources available to me via my Bahamian companies and my Bahamas base, over to California, where my daughter was already a budding property suprema.

As usual, a fresh phase came through a casual contact.

Through a game of golf I met Nat di Carlo, who I very much liked. He had two sides to his business. On one side he held a fund through which he invested money into the stock market. I had no interest in that, but the other side of his business was a commercial real estate, and that did interest me. We agreed to try out a venture or two together.

The first deal we did was for 28 houses spread throughout the Inland Empire of Los Angeles. They were all rented out to third parties, and the controlling investor had some other issues going on elsewhere; he needed to sell. The houses were valued by an independent valuer, and the seller took a 20 percent discount to get out in good time. As the market heated up and the properties climbed sharply in value, his early exit turned out very well for us.

The next development was 12 houses in Rancho Cucamonga, in the foothills of the San Bernardino Mountains. Nat had found a piece of land that was basically a big hole, a storm relief area. Through his and his partner's genius, they found a way to reroute the storm drain underground and get planning for 12 houses. The cost of filling in the hole was much greater than envisaged, but a fantastic deal, nonetheless. Our latest development is for 30 houses in Menifee, another city in the Inland Empire of Los Angeles, which is now booming.

Having now got my feet wet in the US real estate market, I have found a tremendous opportunity in real estate financing, and my next stage is to set up a fund in the Bahamas to take advantage of this.

The future is bright and exciting and I look forward to it very much.

CHAPTER 12

BEST FRIENDS FOREVER

How many people can say, at the age of 50, that their three best friends were all born in the same hospital in the same city in the same year?

I am lucky enough to be able to say so, and Tim, Nick and Nidge have been with me through it all. Along with Julie, they have provided an anchor to my life that's held me steady through all the storms.

When it came to our 50th birthdays, I knew I wanted us all to be together to celebrate.

Even with me leaving the UK in 2007, we still speak at least twice a week, and the attractions of coming to the Bahamas to see me mean they often come out for a visit.

Because our birthdays are clustered close together, we planned to throw a four-day party at a time when two of our actual birthdays would fall on two of the four days, and the other two would pretend that it was his birthday on the other days. Well, it was a very special four days, to say the least, involving 30 friends in total. With a year's planning from me, it turned out to be one of the highlights of my life.

Best friends forever

The first night was a celebration for Nidge, and it was held at Flora Farm. Flora Farm is owned by Patrick and Gloria Greene, two fantastic people and close friends. Flora Farm, up a winding dirt road in the foothills of the Sierra de la Laguna Mountains in San Jose del Cabo, is a little piece of heaven. It includes a restaurant and ten-acre organic farm. Floras Field kitchen makes beautiful, healthy food cooked with ingredients from the farm, served on banquet-style long tables in an impressively large space that is open at the sides to the exquisite riot of flowering plants that surround it. Accommodation takes the form of ten Culinary Cottages, handcrafted luxury outbuildings nestled within a private section. It has become famous as the number one place to go to in Baja, and the most successful restaurant in Mexico.

When we arrived at Flora Farm, I noticed some rather odd-looking covering over all the hay bales that sit around the property as decoration, and elsewhere. I said to Gloria, "Gloria, I can't understand why you've covered all the hay up. And why have you put these plastic sheets everywhere?"

"Lawrence, you'll see," she said.

"Well, you've spoiled the look of it. But it's your call," I replied.

Shaking my head, briefly, I shifted my attention to enjoying what was already shaping up to be a fantastic evening. The theme was Hawaiian, and we had many different bands playing. At midnight, all was revealed about the plastic sheeting. For the first time ever at Flora Farm, there was a huge firework display. Now I understood why Gloria covered up all the hay; the fireworks could have set Flora Farm alight. It was so kind of her to put on the show, especially at a cost of $1,200 a minute for the fireworks!

The second day was my actual birthday. That day, I rented *El Discovery* (aka *SS ShitShow*), the 90-foot boat. We spent the day jet-skiing, paddle-boarding, and partying on the boat. And then in the evening, the entertainment kicked up a notch – a Mariachi band, Brazilian dancers, fire eaters, fire dancers, and then more fireworks. At the climax, the four of us from Sheffield, best mates for decades, performed a full strip to "You Sexy Thing" – the Hot Chocolate song from the film *The Full Monty*. We all ended up in the pool naked. We all, also, blamed cold water as an excuse for what happened to our bodies, even though, in all honesty, the water was warm!

It was probably the best day and night of my life.

The Full Monty

The next day, Day Three, was Nick's party. The guys played golf and the women swam with dolphins where the Pacific Ocean meets the Sea of Cortes. And then, in the afternoon, we all went over to the house of our friend Mike Meldman, the owner of Discovery Properties, and therefore manager of El Dorado, who was described by the *Wall Street Journal* as "real estate's party boy", and claims to be the world's best beer pong player. By his pool, a jazz band played, and we partied the day away.

The final day was Tim's actual birthday. We took over Nikki Beach in Cabo San Lucas – another incredible beach-side complex with open-air dining and views across the sparkling turquoise ocean to dramatic mountains across the bay. We really pulled out all the stops for Tim. We took over the entire main area, including lots of luxurious daybeds, and arranged for several bands to play. One of the highlights was the ceremonial entry of the biggest birthday cake I've ever seen. I have to admit, things got a bit out of hand, and Tim's head ended up stuck in the middle of that cake!! I was very sad to hear that Nikki Beach was devastated by Hurricane Odile in September 2014 and has yet to reopen. It is such a beautiful place.

Later, we walked along the beach to Mango Deck Restaurant and Bar – the site of many drunken Spring Break revelries. There was a live event going on, and we managed to get Tim called up onto the stage to perform a task I had achieved months before: swapping his shorts for his wife's bikini bottoms and then performing a lap dance. Tim being the coward he is, he ran off, dived into the ocean, and left his poor wife bewildered on stage while the show's presenter looked for another unsuspecting victim. By the way, when I was called upon to show off my talents on that earlier occasion, I won!!

It was so special to share my fiftieth birthday with the three people who I've been with since the day I was born. Very, very special indeed.

REFLECTIONS AND THANKS

The chance to live two lives in one life is a real rarity. In my first life, I used all the frustrations from my difficult childhood to throw myself into pursuing some massive goals. With the love of my life, Julie, by my side, I found stability and strength. I wanted to work for the biggest and most-loved brand in the UK, which was Marks & Spencer at the time. After becoming their youngest ever buyer at 24, a year earlier than I could have ever imagined, I threw myself into the challenge of travelling around the world on a shoestring. That could be a whole book within itself.

I landed a shareholding in Café Rouge because I helped someone else, which gave me the chance to watch the share price rise astronomically as we settled back in Sheffield, the home of *The Full Monty*. Hannah and

Toby were born, which was truly the most important thing that ever happened to us.

Who knew that when I decided to buy an ice cream manufacturer, it would lead to me building the fastest-growing restaurant business the UK had ever seen? It changed the face of catering in shopping centres throughout the UK for millions of people. Everything beforehand had been a learning curve for the big one.

The Big Chef was about to become Little Chef. Ever since I left Marks & Spencer, I wanted to own an iconic UK brand. After an incredible start at Little Chef – with the sale and leaseback and the implementation of my business plan – disaster struck. A life-threatening heart attack led me to question whether I would live or die.

I lived, getting the time to reflect on what lessons could be learned to begin a God-given second life against all the odds. The second life has been even more incredible than the first, and there are surely many more chapters to be written.

I have a saying in my office from Abraham Lincoln: "In the end it's not the years in your life that count. It's the life in your years." You've read here the amazing second life I've had the chance to live thus far. My son Toby recently challenged me on what legacy I want to leave behind. I know that it's my two beloved children. I believe that the more time you invest in your children, the more you give to this world for its future. So many people spend so much time doing other things and not bestowing their own children with time to learn from them.

Toby has chosen a completely different career path from anything that I've ever done. He has an astonishingly creative mind. At 23, there is no doubt he has a good chance of becoming an important young film director. He has co-directed and produced a documentary about basketball star Blake Griffin, which explores the relationship Griffin shared with his late best friend Wilson Holloway, who was, in Griffin's words, the most significant inspiration of his life. This documentary is being presented to ESPN for the network's documentary film series, *30 for 30*. If the film is accepted, it will make Toby the youngest ever *30 for 30* director by six years—wow! Toby's other film credits include a music video for Elton John, which Elton featured on his website, and was seen by millions of viewers, and many other music videos for some of the top record labels such as Sony, Columbia Records, Capital Records, and Interscope Records.

After making a BMW commercial which was seen by over one million viewers, Toby has now focused his efforts on investigating rhino poaching in South Africa. Rhino horns are highly sought-after in China and Vietnam and are more valuable than their corresponding weight in gold. Rhino poaching has become a massive problem. Toby's film is of the same ilk as *Blood Diamond*, a movie starring Leonardo DiCaprio, who is also a conservationist and very much interested in what Toby is doing in South Africa.

I can't wait to watch Toby's future, looking in from the outside, and enjoying it all. It's so exciting!

Hannah has always been a winner, and we've always known that she will achieve great things. Her chosen path is commercial real estate. She started her career at CBRE Global Investors, and then moved on to a multifaceted real estate firm. She is still expanding her knowledge and needs a couple more years of experience, but I have no doubt she will take an entrepreneurial route like the one I have followed.

One legacy I know I will be leaving is my latest venture into philanthropy. One of my best friends in Cabo san Lucas, John Pentz, approached me a while back to get involved in his Inspire Mexico charity. After months of hard work, we had a big charity gala and raised $1.5 million in one night—a record in fundraising not just for Cabo San Lucas, but for Mexico as a whole.

We are now in a position to build a 90,000-square-foot building which will house the Boys and Girls Club of Mexico, Gente Joven,

Mobilize Mankind, and Cabo's first food bank. This facility will change the daily lives of 2,000 children and will be a lasting legacy to an area that is dear to my heart.

As this book comes to a close, I want to leave you with my goal when putting this book together. It was my desire to tell the story, the true story, of Little Chef, as so many people have asked for it. In reality though, as I put hundreds of hours into this book, I realized I wanted to tell the story of my trials and tribulations in a way that would be helpful to others. Because of the varied life I've led, I am sure that different people will pick different aspects from my story, and I only hope that whatever aspect that is might help them achieve their life's goals or avoid some of the mistakes that I've made.

I'd also like to thank and acknowledge the important people who have been most influential in both of my lives:

1. My mum was such a special person. She taught my sister and me how to love.

2. Julie has been and still is the rock and stability in my life. She taught me to trust and gave me the confidence to go out and achieve everything in this book and my life.

3. Simon Heath taught me about the importance of details, to leave no stone unturned, and to make sure that everything is covered financially, from all angles. Without Simon, there is no way I could have been so successful.

4. Hannah, my daughter, taught me how to lead but always be there for the weaker ones around you.

5. Toby, my son, taught me that if you encourage, give love and spend time, anything is possible.

6. Dad was influential, as I wanted to prove to him that I could be a success.

7. Nidge is one of my best friends in the world. He has not been as fortunate as me in so many ways, both in love, happiness, and business. But he taught me to always be happy for others and never be jealous of anyone.

8. Tim was always there to listen to my thoughts and help me come to the correct decision, in both my personal and my business life.

9. David Coffer showed me how to buy and sell businesses, as well how to raise finance in doing so.

10. Jane Bownes from Bradwell's taught me how someone could move up from freezing ice cream to become managing director, if only given the chance. So many people are not given the chance to prove what they can do.

11. Richard Drummond taught me that if you tell the truth, you might get into trouble, but you'll never have to lie to cover your lies.

12. Chris Andrew Arthur, a computer genius who was the IT manager at both Out of Town Restaurants and Little Chef, whom I truly loved. Not only was he an IT expert, he was a very special person.

13. Kelvin McGowan was from a poor part of Sheffield. Although he had a rough background, I called him a real diamond in the rough. He was brilliant, and he worked long hours with me, giving so much passion to his work. He transformed the menus for both Out of Town Restaurants and Little Chef. I will always thank him for that.

14. Mark Hurley taught me that a Cockney could actually behave like a northerner!

15. Mickey Carney showed me that it was still possible to make new lifelong friends when you're approaching 50 years old.

16. John Noriega from Tampa taught me to do unto others as you would have done unto yourself.

17. Eddie Healey, the owner of Meadowhall and other various shopping centres, taught me that anybody could realize their dream, and how a little man from the north could become very successful in his chosen field.

18. Elton John taught me how to give back to others less fortunate than myself, and to do it with love.

19. Andre Agassi taught me to give everyone a chance in life.

20. Ian Poulter taught me to never ever give in.

With my heart and soul, Julie

And then, of course, there is Julie. Julie is my heart and soul, my left arm. When I was 17 and she came along, I did not realize that I was not a happy kid. She, and she alone, changed that. She held my hand through the rest of my growing up, the ups and downs at Marks & Spencer, and the trials and tribulations at home with my parents. Looking back on it, travelling together for two years straight, and being together 24 hours a day through that period, was a make or break move for our relationship. And it definitely made us, bonded us together for life, no matter what. Every time I would get involved in a new business with delirious passion and enthusiasm, she would quietly listen, and accepted being dragged around the latest M&S shop, or the new Café Rouge, or the spanking new factory or whatever it was that came across her path as she supported and loved and encouraged me.

At the same time, she was canny enough to give me my space, with time for boys' trips, football outings and all the adventures I've had separately. Julie would never say she is academically accomplished, but she is clever in so many other ways. From when the kids were young through to today, she has been the best mother I have ever seen. She always considers me and made me feel welcome – the whole family would fight to get to the door first to throw their arms around me every time I got home (if it was a reasonable hour!). She has always been there to make me laugh, even if things were getting on top of me, and she was simply amazing all through my heart attack and recovery.

I'm sure most people think I am the boss, but it's not true. Certainly, we have an old-fashioned relationship. I bring home the money and she spends it – only joking! She looks after the house and the kids and it has all worked out fantastically well, with both of us satisfied, stimulated and happy with our lot in life. For the last few years, we have been together nearly as much as when we travelled together for those two years, and the only time we ever have cross words comes because she is always late and I am – like every successful business person I have ever met – extremely punctual. But our disagreements are never serious. We were made for each other – so different, and yet so compatible. I am a very lucky man to have found such a perfect partner so early in life, and to have held onto her.

If I have anyone to thank for the amazing life I have led so far, it is Julie.

CPSIA information can be obtained
at www.ICGtesting.com
Printed in the USA
BVOW10s1754301117
501578BV00009B/217/P